INDIE AUTHOR MAGAZINE

HELLO AND WELCOME!

I'm Indie Annie, and I'm thrilled you're reading this gorgeous full-color version of IAM. Did you know that you can also access all the information, education, and inspiration in our app? It's available on both the iOS App Store and Google Play. And for those that prefer to listen to me read articles, you can pop over to Spotify or our website. Happy Reading!

X

IndieAuthorMagazine.com

Download on the
 App Store

GET IT ON
Google Play

Spotify

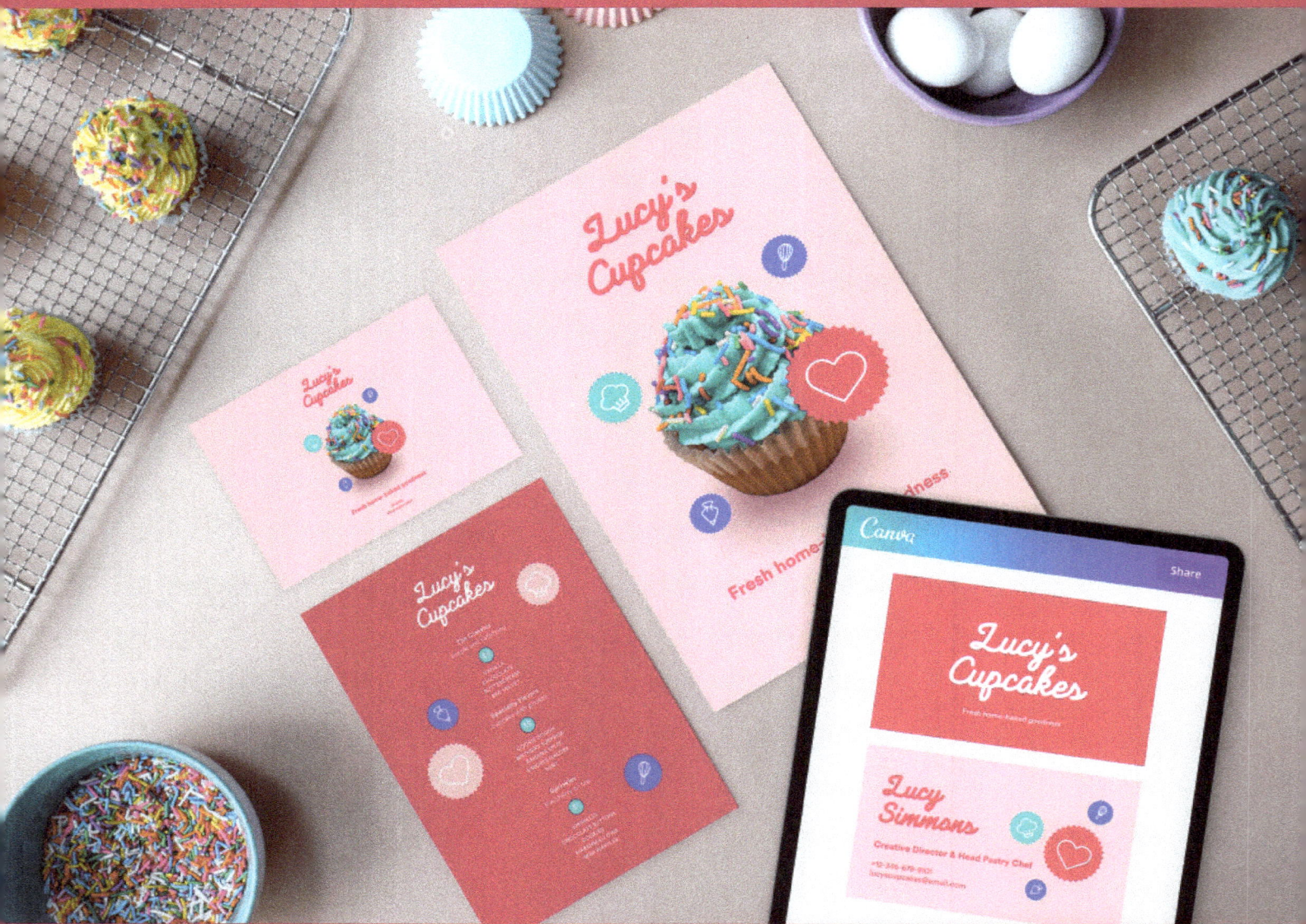

Design like a Pro for free

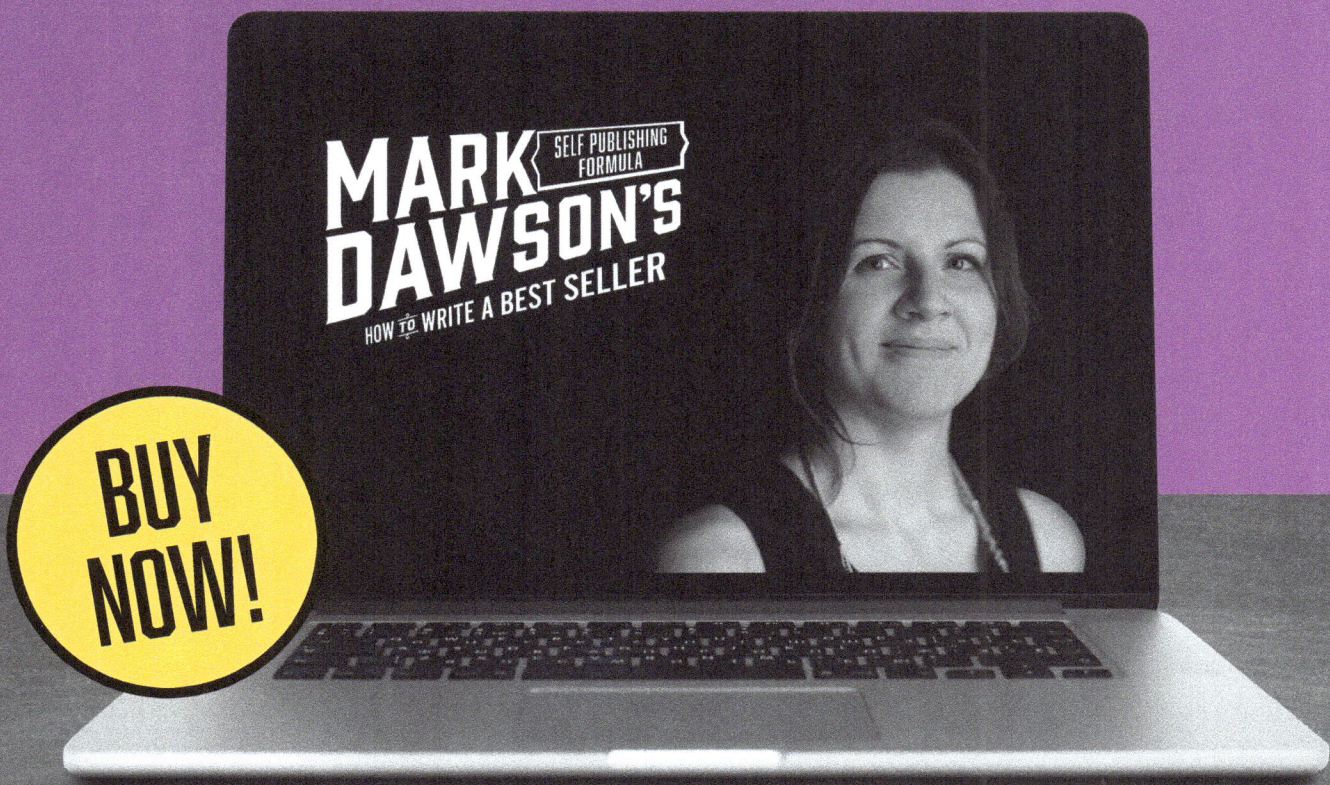

SO YOU WANT TO WRITE A BESTSELLER?

MARK DAWSON'S
SELF PUBLISHING FORMULA
HOW TO WRITE A BEST SELLER

BUY NOW!

JOIN BESTSELLING AUTHOR, SUZY K QUINN, AS SHE REVEALS THE SECRETS BEHIND WRITING A CHART-TOPPING NOVEL.

Tech Takes Center Stage

24

LLCS MADE SIMPLE

What You Need to Know about Starting Your Own Company

30

CHECKS AND BALANCES

When the Royalties Roll in, Here's How Indie Authors Can Budget for the Future

32

5 TIPS FOR MONEY GOALS THAT JUST MAKE CENTS

ON THE COVER

REGULAR COLUMNS

THE WRITE LIFE

TYPEWRITER TALES

INDiE AUTHOR MAGAZINE

PUBLISHER
Chelle Honiker

CREATIVE DIRECTOR
Alice Briggs

EDITOR IN CHIEF
Nicole Schroeder

COPY EDITOR
Lisa Thompson

WRITERS
Angela Archer
Elaine Bateman
Patricia Carr
Bradley Charbonneau
Laurel Decher
Fatima Fayez
Gill Fernley
Greg Fishbone
Chrishaun Keller-Hanna
Jac Harmon
Marion Hermannsen

WRITERS
Kasia Lasinska
Megan Linski-Fox
Bre Lockhart
Sìne Màiri MacDougall
Angie Martin
Merri Maywether
Susan Odev
Jenn Mitchell
Clare Sager
Nicole Schroeder
Emilia Zeeland

PUBLISHER
Athenia Creative
6820 Apus Dr.
Sparks, NV, 89436 USA
775.298.1925

ISSN 2768-7880 (online)–ISSN 2768-7872 (print)

From the Publisher

In the September 2022 issue, I wrote an article about transmedia and how indie authors have the opportunity to capitalize on its facets. Transmedia, at its core, focuses on ways to deepen the relationship you have with your current readers and form new ones. As Jim Wilbourne explains, "Transmedia is taking a core story or core world that your story is built in and then expanding it into different types of media so that different readers or different viewers can experience your world but a different story or experience within that world."

Imagine my surprise when my brilliant daughter, who edited and polished most of the videos for the recent Author Tech Summit, remarked that hosting the summit, and managing its sister site, https://indieauthortools.com, was a form of transmedia for us as a magazine.

And she's right. The magazine is our core work; it's what we feel is our hub. Each month we publish more than two dozen articles digitally, in print, via e-book, on our apps, and in a podcast.

The Author Tech Summit reached a new audience, and it seemed to have struck a chord. More than three-fourths of the 712 participants were new to us, and nearly all of them were new to Indie Author Tools.

By our metrics, that's a successful case study of the power of transmedia in action. We expanded our core audience, and we also introduced our existing readership to something else we offer.

It's always gratifying to see something you've written about come to fruition. Now it's your turn—have you implemented something you've read about in IAM? Email me and let me know!

To Your Success,
Chelle
Publisher
Indie Author Magazine
Email: publisher@indieauthormagazine.com

From the Editor in Chief

I've never considered myself particularly technology capable.

Sure, having grown up awash in new devices and an expanding internet, I'm probably more adept than I give myself credit for. But you can also guarantee I'll need to ask for help from my more computer-savvy friends to set up a website. Over the years, Scrivener and Adobe InDesign have cost me several hours in the form of YouTube tutorials and hopeless clicking. And don't even get me started on social media platforms—in my freshman year of college, my roommate had to give me a crash course on Twitter so I could use it in my reporting class. True story.

All that to say, if you find technology confusing or complicated, you're not alone. The countless tools and applications available to indie authors make our work possible, but even for the strongest tech wizards among us, there are some days when using them can feel downright impossible.

That's why this past month, *Indie Author Magazine* hosted the inaugural Author Tech Summit. Beyond the advice we're able to share in these pages each month, we wanted the chance to dive even deeper into the tools you use daily. As you'll read in this month's cover story, our four-day online event gave more than seven hundred attendees an in-depth look into some of the tools and programs available for every stage of self-publishing. We spoke directly to creators in order to help demystify their platforms, so you could feel more confident clicking through their features and using them to grow your business.

Technology can be tricky, but we also know how important it is for every indie author. So whether it's a 1,200-word article on the most useful features in Draft2Digital, like you'll see in this issue, or a weeklong series of videos exploring platforms from every corner of the writing world, we hope we're able to make those impossible days a little less frequent.

Although I can't speak for anyone else, I know this software amateur appreciates the help.

Nicole Schroeder
Editor in Chief
Indie Author Magazine

PLANNING TRAVEL TO A CONFERENCE?

Use miles.

Time is Money

CONSIDER HOW YOU'RE SPENDING YOUR MOST VALUABLE CURRENCY

Time is the currency of our lives.

We invest it from the moment we're born until our final day. Every moment is given to something that makes us who we are. Your time is the most valuable gift you can give to someone.

Invest in your mind and your soul as they are the foundation of you. Invest in your health. Invest in your family. And finally, invest today's time in your future.

Writing, playing, relaxing, working, and yes, sleeping. As much as I use Facebook, it's not quality time unless I look at it as sifting a stream, panning for gold. There is plenty to be had, as long as I don't waste time with iron pyrite—fool's gold.

Streamlining your processes and becoming efficient with your words are ways to get more from the investment of your time writing a book.

You pay with your time as that becomes money, and money buys the things you don't have time to learn or can't produce for yourself. I buy covers because learning to make them is not something I am equipped for. I don't have time to learn a new trade. I'll invest mine in what I'm good at—writing a story.

And time to give back. Charity is good for my soul, so I give most of mine to charity—time and the money that time has earned for me. I've invested in the future of my family.

Time. The great equalizer. We only have so much of it. Are you using yours to invest wisely in your health and in your future?

The day job is soul-sucking. You write to find a way out of the morass. You're burning the candle at both ends. And then you're free! Do you keep writing? Many struggle with their newfound gift of more time. Stay true to you. Stay true to the path you've laid out with your time investment. You'll invest more, so much more, but will you do it wisely once you have a lot of it?

It's like winning the lottery. Most winners are bankrupt in five years. Such a thing should be inconceivable. But it's not. We don't know what to do with what we don't have, even after we have it.

Time is the currency of your future, spent today. ■

Craig Martelle

Dear Indie Annie,

I'm constantly juggling the writing deadlines I set for myself with the deadlines I need to meet for other people. When others are relying on me to get their work done, my projects always seem to take the back burner. How do I learn to treat my writing with the same importance as the work I do for others?

Conflicted in Columbia

DEAR CONFLICTED,

My dear, yours is a common affliction. Many reading this letter will recognize themselves in your question. I will let you in on a little secret if you promise not to tell anyone else. I suffer from the same disease.

It may come as a shock to my beloved legion of fans, but I too struggle to put my own needs before others. It is a condition I have worked on for decades. I have lost count of the time management and self-help books I have devoured to get some insight into this problem.

I am still a WIP (work in progress), but I am willing to share what has worked for me. These tips come with a health warning though, like any good medication. Taking control of your time and putting yourself and your priorities first can have serious side effects. Regularly saying "no" to others' demands can lead to the loss of friends, contracts, and excuses.

Let me elaborate because knowledge is power, dear Conflicted, and forewarned is forearmed. Knowing about these potential side effects can help you prepare for them when they happen.

Let's begin with one potential side effect: loss of "friends." These so-called friends—and I am talking about managers, colleagues, associates, partners, spouses, and children as well—have grown used to you doing stuff for them. They may not deliberately take advantage of your good nature, but they most certainly have become accustomed to relying on you to deliver.

Am I saying they are all blood-sucking leeches and you should cast them off like dandruff on the shoulders of your black velvet jacket? Absolutely not. But when you start to reevaluate how you manage your priorities, something will have to give. And these "friends" may not like your decisions.

You mentioned how your projects get put on the back burner. You have decided to prioritize other people's work and, as a result, yours has taken a step back. But there are only twen-

Need help from your favorite Indie Aunt?
Ask Dear Indie Annie a question at
IndieAnnie@indieauthormagazine.com

ty-four hours in a day, and you are only human. And unless Hermione Granger is willing to lend you her Time-Turner, they are facts you have to deal with. Once you decide your projects are a higher priority, you will have no choice but to tell other people you can't do something, or you can't do it right now, and that is going to cheese many people off.

I would argue this may well be the reason you have trouble saying no. We're all conditioned to please others. It's not a bad thing. Helping each other makes the world a kinder place to live. But it is easy to lose perspective and balance, and quid pro quo conversations can turn us all into Hannibal Lecter. As you weigh your priorities, you have to decide what value your arrangements hold. If working on your own projects has greater value, consider what else is on the table. It's a business decision. Look at the facts and take the emotion out of it. I am not suggesting you morph into a selfish Billy-no-mates, as there are enough of them in the world already. I am saying you have to review constantly and understand that some things may need to be renegotiated.

This may be harder when it comes to your contracted deadlines. Again, you need to determine the value of those contracts. Are they unrealistic? Are you being fairly recompensed for your time and expertise? If not, can you rework your agree-

ment? Sometimes we cling to things out of fear. And a loss of income is scary. In the current climate, it's arguably worse than losing your "friends." But sometimes you must take a leap of faith. I am not going to counsel you to give up the day job because only you know your financial position, but if you need the security of a salary or are committed to a series of low-paying freelance gigs, then until you are in a position to break away, other things in your life may need to take a back seat so you have time to write or market your own books.

Once you have evaluated your time sucks, the only things left to lose are your excuses. And dear Conflicted, this is the hardest loss of all. Imagine a life where there are no obstacles getting in the way of your genius. A clear path freshly weeded and newly paved for you to stride along. Nothing to trip you up; no one to hold you back. You are Usain Bolt lining up for the hundred-meter sprint. The finish line is in your sights. Are you going to visualize your end goal and run toward it, or are you going to faff around, retying your shoelaces for the tenth time?

The expectations of friends and the requirements of contracts are reasons you have to put your project aside until later. There may be other reasons, like ill health or lack of resources. Maybe you took a wrong turn in Bogotá and are currently

Continued on page 17

10 TIPS FOR
DRAFT2DIGITAL

Indie authors often consider the valid option of going wide and publishing on other platforms beyond Amazon. But with it comes a lot of work adapting your book formatting and spending time uploading to multiple platforms. At least, it used to.

Draft2Digital is a self-publishing aggregator, allowing authors to publish a book automatically on multiple online retailers. Instead of creating an account and uploading your book to each individual site, you can let Draft2Digital do all the hard work for you, including managing all the different formatting standards for each distributor.

Sounds positively magical, doesn't it? And by and large, for authors who want to publish wide, it is. Below, we'll talk you through just some of the features of Draft2Digital that help increase sales, save time, and make author life easier. You'll then have the needed information to decide whether D2D is the best option for you.

1 PUBLISH ACROSS MULTIPLE PLATFORMS

Without getting into an exclusive-or-wide debate, suffice it to say that Draft2Digital can get your books—both e-book and print—into a whole slew of online stores, as well as libraries and physical stores. As the author, you also get to choose where your book is distributed, so you have complete control without spending hours uploading your books to multiple individual sites. That might be fun when you're all excited over book one, but it can get old really fast by the time you're uploading book number thirty.

Pro Tip: With Draft2Digital, you can set the price for your book to zero dollars. This is really helpful if you want a perma-free book on Amazon as you can now get them to price match.

2 QUICKLY AND EASILY FORMAT FOR E-BOOK AND PRINT

Use Draft2Digital's formatting tool to produce a high-quality copy of your book that's ready for both e-book and print. The platform doesn't have any formatting restrictions, and it can work with almost any layout you have. The program does have guidelines, such as using the same formatting every time you do a chapter heading so it stands out but is simple to use.

The program offers several options for the final layout and allows you to choose between PDF and EPUB file formats. You can also preview the work before you publish to make sure it looks right. And if you already have a formatted copy of your book, the program will accept that too. It's all very straightforward.

3 SAVE MONEY WHEN STARTING OUT

When using Draft2Digital, you don't pay a subscription fee, and there are no hidden charges. Draft2Digital simply charges 10 percent of your royalties on each book you sell in addition to whatever cut each online store takes. You'll usually end up with around 60 percent royalties for your e-books and 45 percent royalties for print. In effect, you don't pay until you've made a sale.

This can be a cost-effective way to get started if you're new to self-publishing. You don't have to pay a formatter. You don't have to pay for distribution. You just upload and publish, then get paid each month, depending on your payment settings, minus the online store's and Draft2Digital's cuts.

4 CREATE UNIVERSAL BOOK LINKS

If you sell books in multiple stores, you want every reader to be able to choose the best store for them. You can either attempt to list all the links to every store individually, or you can use Draft2Digital's Universal Book Link (UBL).

Paste a link to your book on Draft2Digital (https://books2read.com/links/ubl/create), and Draft2Digital will search for every instance of your book on every online store. It will then create a single link for your book. Change the name of the link to your book name to remove the string of random characters and make the URL easier for readers to remember. When readers click on it, they can then choose which shop they want to buy your book from, giving you a greater chance of making a sale at their preferred outlet.

5 PROMOTE YOURSELF WITH YOUR AUTHOR PAGE

Every author who uses Draft2Digital gets an editable author page where readers can find their bio, photo, and all of their books with a UBL to every distribution channel.

You can also include your social media links, and there's a button for readers to sign up for your mailing list or get new release notifications.

You can customize your author page to suit you, and it's entirely geared toward selling your books. Although you may already have a website with this information, it never hurts to have another place where you can show off your books.

6 HIGHLIGHT INDIVIDUAL BOOKS WITH BOOK TABS

Book tabs give readers all the information they need for a single book. The customizable tab includes the book cover, blurb, series title, and your author image and bio.

Even better, the webpage includes a UBL that lets readers choose their preferred store, thumbnail covers for the rest of the series, a link to more of your books, and links to follow you on social media, sign up for your newsletter, or get new release notifications.

This could be a really useful page to share on release day and in ongoing promotions.

7 SET UP PREORDERS

You can set up preorders for both e-book and print books a year in advance on every store except Amazon, where it's not possible to do a preorder for e-books. You don't even need to have your cover or a placeholder file to do so. In fact, Draft2Digital recommends that you don't use a placeholder file at all.

You'll just need to upload your cover and final file ten days before your release day at the latest.

8 SPLIT ROYALTIES AUTOMATICALLY

If you've ever written with a co-writer or organized an anthology with several writers, you know what a challenge it is to keep up with the royalties, split them equally for each author, and manage your accounts. This is especially true if you've published on multiple platforms.

Save yourself a lot of work by getting each co-author to sign up with Draft2Digital, and then you can specify what percentage of the royalties each author gets. After that, everything is automatically paid for you, and you'll have only one platform to look at when it comes to your company accounts.

9 CREATE AUTOMATED END MATTER

How many times have you formatted a book and had to recreate the front matter and back matter from scratch?

With Draft2Digital's formatter, you won't have to worry about it again. You don't need to include a title page or a copyright page as they'll automatically set that up for you. Save your back matter when you set up your first book, and every time you release a new book or update your bio, you can update your back matter too. The site will carry over the update to every book you've published. For authors who have published several books, this is a massive time saver.

If you've yet to publish, start off by saving your back matter and then keep updating it. You'll thank yourself, and Draft2Digital, every time you have a new release and don't have to repeatedly update your end matter for every book.

10 WATCH FOR NEW FEATURES IN THE COMING YEAR

In March 2022, Draft2Digital acquired Smashwords, another large self-publishing aggregator. Although the companies are still working on integrating, the general consensus within the indie author world is that this could be great news for authors who use the platforms.

So far, the companies have announced that Draft2Digital authors will be able to publish in the Smashwords Store, which pays 80 percent royalties, once the integration is complete. You'll also be able to issue Smashwords coupons and use book marketing tools from Smashwords, including the Smashwords presales tool.

These are just some of the benefits of using Draft2Digital. But is the site right for your author business?

Certain online stores offer better options to authors that publish directly with them rather than through an aggregator. You may want to publish directly with Kobo, iTunes, Amazon, and Barnes & Noble, then publish through Draft2Digital for every other store so that you still have access to smaller distributors without uploading each one individually.

Here's what to think about:

How long will it take you to manage all the formatting requirements and publish directly to those four platforms along with Draft2Digital? Are the extras and options you get on those platforms worth that extra effort to you? Or would you rather skip the options, save the extra time and energy, and publish to all platforms via Draft2Digital? Only you know what you're prepared to do and which option will best suit you and your author business.

And that's perhaps the greatest part about the platform! Draft2Digital gives you some excellent options, and you get to choose what's best for you. ■

Gill Fernley

DEAR INDIE ANNIE CONTINUES...

waiting for a garage to fix your flat tire, and there's no Wi-Fi for miles. But everything else is an excuse.

Let me tell you, I am the queen of making excuses. I'm a veritable Empress of Procrastination. And the secret I have discovered to beating excuses is to slay them one by one, over and over, like a lifelong game of Whac-a-Mole. In every precious moment you have negotiated back to yourself, you need to write.

Everyone has commitments. Everyone has responsibilities. Everyone is busy. But successful people value themselves and their time. They honor the minutes, hours, and days by filling them with activities that propel them forward.

They understand that, in every moment, they have a choice. And they always aim to do the right thing at the right time. Sometimes the right thing is to do something for others. Sometimes it is to do something for yourself. And sometimes it is to do nothing at all.

The key word is balance. Balance in all things. Achieve that, and yes, you might lose stuff along the way, but think of all you could gain.

Happy writing,
Indie Annie

Tech Takes Center Stage at IAM's First Author Tech Summit

Just one facet of being a published indie author is universal, and that is technology.

You are free to choose the genre, the tropes, and the story arc of every work you produce. You're able to choose how words appear on the page—whether that means filling notebooks with prose, speaking the story aloud into a dictation program, or banging out hundred-thousand-word tomes on a keyboard. You're free to choose whether it is a solo endeavor to get your book from ideation to publication or whether you will employ editors, virtual assistants, formatters, designers, or marketing staff to help.

But you'll need technology to publish, market, and sell your work—and it was that one uniting factor for all modern published authors that inspired the inaugural Author Tech Summit, hosted virtually by *Indie Author Magazine* this past month, September 13-16.

The four-day event was free to attendees, with sessions available for twenty-four hours, so participants could view them in any order and at any time, from any time zone. Sessions were dedicated to hands-on demonstrations of popular tools and an under-the-hood look at ways to optimize an author's technology engine, with each day's theme corresponding to a different step in the writing and publishing process. Discussions included everything from story development to social media marketing, all with the goal of helping make technology more accessible to as many authors as possible. And at least by the numbers, one could argue it succeeded—during the four days of the live event, over seven hundred students watched more than 41,000 minutes of video.

Worried you missed out? Don't fret—we've summed up everything you might have missed from the summit below. If you want to learn more, replays of the sessions are available at https://authortechsummit.com by purchasing an all-access pass for $197, which opens up access for an entire year and includes additional bonus sessions.

AUTHOR ·TECH· SUMMIT

DAY ONE: READER ENGAGEMENT AND STORY DEVELOPMENT

Day one of the summit launched with sessions from four different apps that help authors build their world, write their manuscripts, format them, and find new readers.

WORLD ANVIL

Janet Forbes, CEO and co-founder of World Anvil, took participants on a tour of the world-building and novel-writing software, which was created by her husband for her to finish her "unfinishable" novel. World Anvil, originally aimed at gamers and fantasy writers for its ability to create maps and fleshed-out worlds, also presented a second session that showed practical applications for authors using its time-line builder, character templates, and manuscript-writing tool.

REEDSY

Reedsy is best known for the online directory of editing, design, and other professionals, but in this session, Reedsy's Ricardo Fayet introduced the software's writing and formatting tool called Reedsy Book Editor, highlighting the features of the online tool and demonstrating one key feature sure to be popular: collaboration, allowing co-authors and editors to share a document without overriding one another's work.

KICKSTARTER

Kickstarter has garnered a lot of attention in recent months after Brandon Sanderson's record-breaking campaign raised the most money ever by any user on the platform. Two Kickstarter sessions led participants through the basics of the app, including ways to get started with Kickstarter led by the company's director of publishing and comics outreach, Oriana Leckert, and a deeper dive into building a sales page campaign from Russell Nohelty and Monica Leonelle, bestselling co-authors of the indie author guidebook *Get Your Book Selling on Kickstarter*.

PLOTTR

Plottr is a visual outline and story bible tool for writers. In this session, Ryan Zee, co-founder and head of marketing, and Troy Lambert, education lead for the program, talked with Author Tech Summit Director of Operations Amy Holiday about how discovery writers—or those who aren't plotters by nature—can utilize the program. Zee and Lambert delved into four concepts, including post-plotting, revising first drafts, managing story and series bibles, and tracking tent-pole events.

DAY TWO: CONTENT MANAGEMENT

Day two focused on ways for authors to reach readers in new ways using websites, podcasts, and text-to-speech and translation tools to generate marketing materials.

GOOGLE RICH SNIPPETS

Rich snippets are panels of information displayed in search results, offering audiences expanded information about the book, author, links to libraries, and links to buy. This session described how indie authors can use their website and other resources to alert Google to display this information using schemas, machine-readable formatting standard to most websites.

HOW TO WRITE BLOG POSTS THAT UPDATE ELSEWHERE

Using the power of RSS feeds, this session walked participants through the steps of writing a blog post and formatting its machine-readable template with links, images, and excerpts so that it can be used to populate newsletters, author profile pages, search results, push notifications, and social media posts.

AI MARKETING VIDEOS

Artificial intelligence (AI) tools for text-to-speech have become sophisticated enough for use in everyday marketing efforts. This session presented a use-case of creating sound files with two characters' dialogue "spoken" using AI and combined into a short-form video for use on platforms like TikTok or Instagram.

AUTOMATIC AMAZON AUTHOR PAGE AND GOODREADS PROFILE UPDATES

Building on the "Blog Once and Update Everywhere" session, this presentation delved deeper into the specifics of how to automate updates to the author's profiles on Amazon and Goodreads using an RSS feed from each of the major website platforms.

ANCHOR.FM

Anchor.FM is a podcasting tool that serves as a central point for creating, editing, and syndicating podcasts. This session explored the possibilities of using Anchor.FM in two ways. The first described the steps for indie authors wanting to publish audio versions of serial fiction with ads or listener support. The second showed authors how to upload AI-generated sound files to produce a podcast and syndicate it to Google Play, Amazon Music, Apple Podcasts, and other podcast download sites.

A PRO EDITOR'S TIPS FOR RECORDING YOUR OWN AUDIOBOOK

Not every author can afford to hire a narrator, but with the right setup and know-how, almost any author can produce a quality audio edition of their work on their own. Professional audiobook editor Jim Wilbourne walked attendees through setting up an advanced sound file editor and detailed what he does to ensure a raw recorded sound file has all the technical aspects required to achieve a polished result.

DAY THREE: EMAIL SERVICE PROVIDERS

Each of the email service providers profiled on day three—Sendy, Sendinblue, Mailchimp, MailPoet, MailerLite, and SendFox—was selected for features advantageous to indie authors. Presentations highlighted the basics of each, along with more advanced automation and other tricks for experienced users in additional sessions. Below are standout features for each platform that were highlighted.

SENDY

- Installed on a website host and configured to send emails like other email service providers
- Instead of logging into a service, the author hosts and controls their own newsletter service with most of the same features as other paid services
- $69 for one website and hosting

SENDINBLUE

- Charges for emails sent rather than per subscriber
- Integrated with websites for instant follow-up emails based on visitor activity
- Excellent choice for authors selling direct

MAILCHIMP

- Free version still available
- Great for automating newsletters using RSS feeds

MAILPOET

- Installed on WordPress websites as plugin
- Owned by WooCommerce, with exclusive features as a result
- Subscriber lists remain on the website for optimized data control
- Free up to one thousand subscribers

MAILERLITE

- Survey option can be used to ethically direct higher reviews to sites
- Zapier can be used to send notifications and attachments

SENDFOX

- Attractive one-time payment for lifetime access
- Smart Campaigns can automate newsletter sending
- Rounding out the event, five sessions gave participants specific steps to manage social media posts and channels, as well as tips to engage readers more deeply.

DAY FOUR: SOCIAL MEDIA SCHEDULING

SOCIAL MEDIA MAGIC AND WIZARDRY

Indie Author Magazine Creative Director Alice Briggs taught two sessions using common spreadsheet tools to help streamline social media scheduling across multiple channels. She included tips for how to choose which channels to focus on and how to create images in batches to save steps and time.

HOOTSUITE APPS

Hootsuite, at its core, is a social media planning and monitoring app. Its free version includes a feature that incorporates third-party apps, which participants learned are ways to find new content, monitor TikTok trends, and create graphics in Canva without leaving the app.

PROMOREPUBLIC

In this session, attendees explored another social media posting tool, PromoRepublic, and its key features that give users an all-in-one planning calendar and more advanced graphic design options.

ZAPIER HACKS

Zapier is an application that connects other apps using the concept of "workflows." This advanced session showcased how to add subscriber data into an email service provider to send targeted email; how to keep email subscriber lists backed up and able to import elsewhere; how to validate email addresses before adding to a primary list; how to send social media updates by entering information into a blog post or Google Sheet, and how to manage monthly paid subscriptions and downloads.

Organizers for Author Tech Summit are already planning another event for January 2023 with a focus on website design, graphic design applications, and tools that authors use to distribute wide and sell from their own websites. Register for email updates at https://authortechsummit.com. ◾

IAM Staff

LLCs Made Simple

WHAT YOU NEED TO KNOW ABOUT STARTING YOUR OWN COMPANY

I recently was working with an author on a project to refresh her brand and organize her business. In addition to a fresh start, she wanted to separate her business from her personal assets for the rebranding. Sure, she could have done all this within her existing Kindle Direct Publishing account, but she wanted to take her business to the next level.

After some discussion, we decided it was time for her to create a limited liability company (LLC) for her work.

After incorporating the LLC, the author I worked with began relaunching books under a new pen name within the company. This new company has its own tax ID, bank account, and publishing accounts on all the major platforms.

You're not alone if legal jargon and filing fees make creating an LLC sound complicated. Plenty of authors debate the need for a separate company when they already publish their work as an individual. But the decision to create one can have financial and tax implications, especially if you already have an established author business. Maybe that's you, or maybe it's still early. But if your writing is more than a hobby, you need to understand the process and the pros and cons behind it nonetheless.

WHAT IS AN LLC?

An LLC is a charter from a state that identifies certain assets, liabilities, and activities as separate from you and your personal assets and liabilities. An LLC also has a special agreement called an operating agreement that sets a company's rules. The operating agreement is flexible and can outline ownership, various rules and responsibilities, and how succession works. The federal government has legally established that companies are separate legal individuals for all intents and purposes. So the agreement explains to everyone how this company operates on its own.

This designation and separation provides you with protection. In the worst case of some legal trouble, including a bankruptcy filing, your personal assets are separate and won't have any claims made against them—only the business assets will be at risk.

WHY FORM AN LLC?

Before I answer that question, it's essential to understand that my advice to authors is based on the premise that you want to build a successful full-time career selling your content while working with limited resources. These authors should take steps in the correct order to make the most of the resources they're investing in their business.

Your writing is a career, not a hobby. You may not be making any money, but you're going to spend money to get this enterprise going, and your journey will ideally result in a profitable business built around the content you create. Over the course of writing and publishing your work, you might pay for courses and subscriptions, hire cover designers, or purchase software to write or edit—and in the process, according to the Internal Revenue Service, you are accumulating expenses as a sole proprietor.

Now, this article isn't about taxes, nor is this tax advice. I'm establishing the ground rules of entrepreneurship in the United States, but as you earn more profits, companies—when set up correctly—provide some tax advantages over a sole proprietorship.

As far as the IRS is concerned, you can operate as a sole proprietor, accumulating expenses and charging them against your gross profits to determine your net profit. But the IRS expects you to pay federal income and self-employment taxes on that net profit.

In the beginning, when you're not profitable, you can claim those expenses against other income to lower your tax liability. In essence, you get to charge the business loss during start-up against income you earn elsewhere, like at your day job. Even if you set up an LLC, nothing changes from a tax perspective without a special tax election. A standard LLC is called a pass-through entity, and it's treated just like a sole proprietor.

However, as a sole proprietor, your business activities, assets, and liabilities are connected. If you could not pay your bills and creditors sought repayment, including state and federal tax authorities, they could make claims against your existing personal assets to get paid. Simply put, if you were sued and lost the case, the court could put a lien against your home and other personal assets. But a company creates a different legal bucket of assets and liabilities. The creation of a company sets up a separate entity that the state and the federal government see as assets and liabilities distinct from your personal ones. It's in the name—limited liability.

WHEN SHOULD I SET UP AN LLC OR INCORPORATE A COMPANY?

For some, setting up a company and separating personal and business assets is one of the first steps of any start-up business, including a publishing house.

My approach with authors is a little different. Instead of focusing on the trappings of a business, I consider its success. Paying to incorporate your company before you even write your first book creates a legally recognized company, but it does nothing to help that business succeed. If you're strapped for cash, paying to set up the business

could even harm your chances of success. Starting fees for LLCs can range from 50 to 150 dollars, according to underlined entrepreneurial information service Start Filing (https://start-filing.com/llc-fees) with some states requiring several hundred dollars annually in additional fees. If you spend that money at the beginning of your author journey, you can't use it on something that could instead help bring your product to market.

Setting up a company also creates additional paperwork and fees. You may have to file a separate tax return, and in most states, you will need to pay an annual fee and file a registration form. This is why I suggest looking at setting up your company only after your business has cleared the hurdle of earning ten thousand dollars a year in profit. Doing so before earning that much means you are spending a large percentage of your expenses on accounting and state fees just to maintain the company's standing, and none of that work or money ever contributes to selling a single book.

Of course, there are exceptions to waiting. If you plan to collaborate with others or are going to be writing controversial content or content that comes with an added risk, you could benefit from setting up a company and separating your assets, even from another company you may have or for an operating agreement and separate investment.

So when should you set up an LLC? I think if you earn more than ten thousand dollars in net profit, are in a partnership with another author, or are involved in higher-risk activities, then it's time to get your LLC chartered.

WHICH DO I NEED: AN LLC OR A CORPORATION?

Once you decide it's time to create an LLC, visit the website of the Secretary of State in the state where you reside. Here, you can find information as to the different types of companies that you can charter and the associated costs. There are usually two main types: an LLC and a corporation. Both create a separate legal entity from you

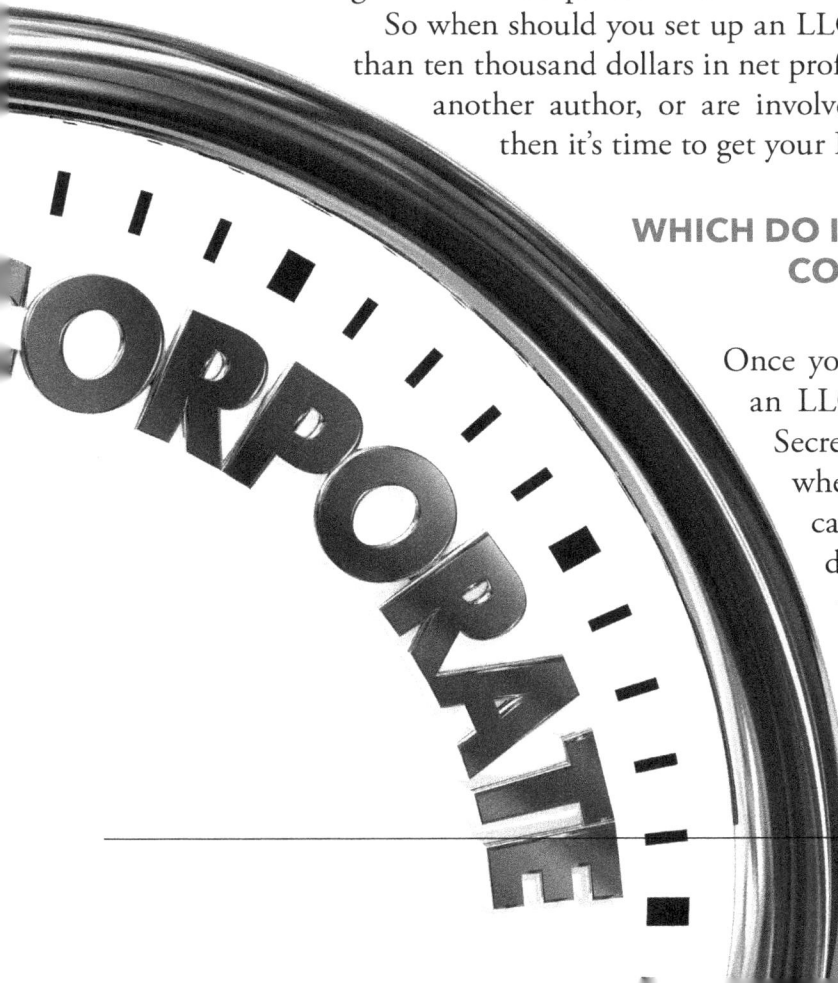

personally. The difference is how the entities are managed and how equity is structured.

For an LLC, you create an operating agreement, or the rules of operation, which can be very flexible. In that agreement, capital is also defined, which allows you to form different types of membership for your LLC, with different rules as to other individuals' ownership in the company and how they receive profits.

A corporation is much more rigid in its structure. Stockholders have ownership in the company, and each share translates to equal claim on assets as any other. Most states require you to have a named board member or board members who manage the business. The board is elected by shareholders, though shareholders typically don't manage the business. This structure is designed for joint ownership by non-operating partners.

In some states, such as Massachusetts, sole operators choose to set up corporations because they come with fewer fees. However, in most states, an LLC is the most cost-effective and easiest company to create.

WHAT'S THIS S-CORP THING?

You may hear people say they have an S-Corp. This isn't an entity like an LLC or a corporation, but it is a tax designation for those entities. An LLC is considered a pass-through entity, which means its profits flow through to your personal tax return and are taxed at your nominal tax rate. A corporation, on the other hand, currently has a federal corporate income tax, and the dividends you take out are taxed at your personal tax rate, resulting in double taxation.

The IRS allows you to get permission for special tax treatment, called a Subchapter S tax election, which is a hybrid tax treatment and gives you the best tax treatment in most cases. Create an LLC and ask the IRS to treat it as an S-Corporation, and you might save money when it comes to your company's tax bills each year. ■

Joe Solari

TYPES OF ORGANIZING STRUCTURES

SOLE PROPRIETOR

WHAT IS IT?

How the IRS designates earning a profit outside of a wage on a W-2 tax form

WHEN TO USE IT?

You are automatically considered a sole proprietor if you are earning income that is not wages.

LIMITED LIABILITY COMPANY

WHAT IS IT?

A legal entity that holds assets and liabilities and becomes a vehicle for conducting business

WHEN TO USE IT?

When you earn more than $10,000 in net profit, are in a partnership with another author, or are involved in high-risk activities

CORPORATION

WHAT IS IT?

A legal entity that holds assets and liabilities and becomes a vehicle for conducting business. This type of company has an alternative management and equity structure with a joint stock basis and a board for control.

WHEN TO USE IT?

If you live in a state where LLCs don't exist or are more expensive

S-CORP ELECTION

WHAT IS IT?

A special tax designation that is applied to small private LLCs or corporations and creates a tax advantage over pass-through taxation

WHEN TO USE IT?

When you set up your LLC, it might be more cost efficient to be treated as an S-Corp. Consult with a tax consultant in your jurisdiction.

Checks and Balances

WHEN THE ROYALTIES ROLL IN, HERE'S HOW INDIE AUTHORS CAN BUDGET FOR THE FUTURE

June 2022 was a record-setting month for the United States economy—and not in the way anyone was hoping. A combination of factors, including the COVID-19 pandemic, Russia's invasion of Ukraine, and continuing supply-chain shortages, drove the country's inflation rate to 9.1 percent, the highest seen in forty years. And we're not alone. Other countries around the world have also experienced rising inflation rates this year, according to Statista, for many of the same reasons.

For a number of people, the trend has reiterated a need to monitor spending now in order to save for tougher months down the road. It can be an important practice for anyone, but especially for those who are self-employed or manage small businesses, writes Mari Ramirez, owner of Open Bookkeeping, a full-service accounting firm in Austin, Texas. Whether the client is a startup with an initial investment or an individual's self-managed business,

Ramirez has seen a variety of companies drain funds quickly simply by not tracking their finances. "There are plenty of reasons why businesses fail; one of the biggest I see is (not) planning and budgeting."

Whatever goals you have for your author business, reinvesting in yourself and your work will help you understand where you are now as well as develop more clear goals for the future, according to the Better Business Bureau. Consider it another way: You can be a "pantser" when writing, but you shouldn't be one when it comes to finances. Don't let this outline stress you out too much, though—before you break out the spreadsheets and calculators, we have a few tips for you to keep in mind.

KEEP YOUR BOOKS BALANCED

Before you worry about dividing your funds to save, invest, or spend, you need to know your current money situation. That means balancing your books—and no, not the ones on your shelf.

Beyond just keeping track of your earnings each month, a profit and loss statement can help you understand your business' net income over a set time period, and a balance sheet can help you calculate the assets and liabilities—cash or inventory and debts—of your business at a particular moment, according to the US Small Business Administration (SBA). The simplest versions of the statements sort and label income streams and expenses within a given time frame—these SCORE profit and loss statement and balance sheet templates, found on the SBA website (https://sba.gov), can be a good place to start.

First, decide how often you'd like to evaluate your funds—monthly, quarterly, or annually, for example—but consider a time span that evenly divides a year and reflects how often you release new titles. A shorter evaluation window can help you understand cash flow trends and track the success of new business strategies, such as an additional marketing tactic or new ad campaign, but a longer window that stretches from one release until the next will incorporate the ebb and flow of new sales and provide a better sense of your overall financial situation.

As you begin to track your earnings and expenses, be thorough: Include the cost of editors, covers, ads, and other production costs, but also include annual software subscriptions, office supplies, and business development expenses, such as conferences or writing workshops you attend. Also keep in mind that your net income won't always equate to your current cash balance—what you have in the bank at the current moment, Ramirez writes. "Net income ties to the balance sheet and cash is only one part of the balance sheet, so it doesn't give you the entire picture." Although knowing your net income will be important to understanding the health of your business, both numbers will play into how you construct goals and budget for future investments.

THE '50-30-20' METHOD

Once you understand how much money you regularly spend and receive, it's time to develop a budget based on the results. Your process should be reasonable to understand and maintain long term, so choose the method that works best for you—and

if you're unsure what that might be, the "50-30-20" method could be a good place to start, according to CNBC and the Creative's CFO, a financial resource for entrepreneurs.

The budgeting method, popularized by Senator Elizabeth Warren in her book *All Your Worth: The Ultimate Lifetime Money Plan*, separates profits on a monthly basis according to percentages of one's profit. The way those amounts are allocated vary based on whether the budget is meant for one's own earnings or for a business. For the latter, professionals at Creative's CFO recommend assigning 50 percent to your personal salary, 30 percent to taxes, and the remaining 20 percent to saving and/or reinvesting in your business. For an author, that could include a re-release with updated covers, new merchandise for fans, or even a ticket to that writing retreat you've been eyeing.

From there, consider taking a portion of the money to form an additional rainy day fund. According to the investment service Motley Fool, emergency savings can be just as important for businesses as they are for individuals, providing security in case of natural disasters, tougher economic environments, or other unforeseen circumstances. Keep the money separate from other long-term savings, according to Motley Fool, so as not to deplete your emergency funds when making a planned investment or your business' nest egg during a financial hardship. Even if you end up needing to dip into your long-term savings account, your emergency funds will help provide extra security and ideally mean less stress on your shoulders during challenging times.

TIME IS MONEY

However you decide to budget, keep your process simple. Your time is valuable as an author, as it is with any business, and managing your finances shouldn't be so complicated that it takes away opportunities to earn more.

As you organize your finances, consider keeping business earnings and expenditures in a separate account from your personal savings. The shift will make keeping track of your income easier, including for tax documents, according to *Publisher's Weekly*, and will save time as you calculate future profit and loss statements. You don't even need to wait until you meet your local bank's qualifications for a business account. Some online payment processors, such as PayPal or Square, can serve as safe places to store funds without a minimum balance while offering similar features to a business checking account.

Finally, whatever process you decide for budgeting your business earnings, be flexible. "Reevaluating your budget and your goals is just as important as creating them to begin with," Ramirez writes. "See where you are falling behind or where you need to improve." As your earnings or expenses fluctuate over time, or as your business expands, your budgeting plan might need to adapt as well—by allocating more money toward savings, for example, or by decreasing the amount you pay yourself in better months in order to grow your emergency fund.

Fortunately or unfortunately, there's no one right answer for how to budget, so find out what makes sense for your author business. Even if that involves hiring an accountant or other financial advisor down the line, Ramirez writes, simply organizing your payments and creating a professional plan for how to handle finances is already an important first step—one that can only benefit you. "I would say that money management is probably one of the most important things in knowing the health of a small business," she writes. "From your budget, you can create a plan for the future, not only for your business but for yourself." ■

Nicole Schroeder

5 Tips for Money Goals that Just Make Cents

Indie authors face numerous challenges: the ever-changing landscape of social media platforms, suppressed visibility, the constant battle to get their books in front of readers' faces, marketing woes, and more. How can you tell whether you're making any progress in your career?

When it comes to the business side of publishing, hitting monetary milestones can allow you to gauge some sense of growth. But how should you approach setting these financial goals for your business—and how can you be sure they're attainable?

Before looking ahead, you need to know where you're starting. We've put together a list of five tips to help you figure out where your business is now in order to direct its future.

1. FIND YOUR WHY

"Knowing your 'why' is crucial." —Katie Forrest, author of *Time Management for Writers*

It's important to note from the outset that each author's business—and their motivation for publishing—looks different. There's no one-size-fits-all version of success, so treat your research as an advice buffet, presented for you to cherry pick what might work for your own business.

The same is true when it comes to setting financial goals. First, understand what drives you to self-publish. Are you writing for fun? Do you want to work your way out of a day job? Do you just want some extra money to supplement your income, or does your household depend on the monthly royalties you receive? How you approach your business will vary based on your core motivation.

2. QUESTION THE PREMISE

"Creative goals are for authors. Business goals are for publishers. If you are an indie author, you are both." —Erika Everest, author of *The Strategic Author's Guide to Mailerlite*

In her book, *Dear Writer, You Need to Quit*, Becca Syme suggests that indie authors need to question the premise of what they are facing before diving into the unknown. Let's consider her advice: Why should indie authors need to set monetary goals for their businesses in the first place?

Business goals, which increase your bottom line, serve a different purpose than creative goals, which shape your brand. Creative goals don't always correlate with more income, and they don't always allow you to consider your work as a product.

Authors who aren't as savvy with the business side of publishing should especially focus on setting business goals. That doesn't mean you have to find an agent or go the traditional publishing route. Set monetary goals when self-publishing, and you'll be able to critically view your work for its value to readers rather than its value to you as the author. You'll have more opportunity to spot weaknesses on the business side of publishing and decide what to change about your writing process or your author brand ahead of time to keep your audience invested.

By having goals on the business side of your career, you can shift your writing from hobbyist to professional. And without measurable goals, you can't gauge growth. "It's a mindset change," says Contemporary Romance author Tracie Delaney, "and one that not enough focus is put on."

3. DECIDE WHAT SUCCESS LOOKS LIKE

"Success isn't glamorous. Success is dedication and consistency over time. If you're hitting someone else's yard stick, it can feel like you're failing." —Meg Jolly, British Crime author

Don't set goals in a vacuum. You will feel inadequate if you write down a list of arbitrary targets that are someone else's and don't mean anything to you.

Think about how you define success. Is it a certain number of books sold? A specific monthly income? Is it the ability to work a half day and spend more time with your family while earning the same amount of money?

Financial goals need to be linked to tangible benefits and concrete targets. Otherwise, the money is meaningless, and you will keep chasing it blindly. Instead of choosing an arbitrary amount to strive for, decide what you wish to achieve with that money, such as turning your writing into a full-time career, and calculate goals from there. This mindset will help to break the goal into more manageable steps, but it will also help you weigh the value of that money against your other priorities, such as family time or your health.

We could all make more money or write more books if we invested more time and effort, but only you can decide whether that time and effort is worth the personal price you will pay.

4. BREAK IT DOWN

"Goals are like jet fuel. If you have nothing to aim at, it's easy to wander or just stay at one level. My first goal was to have no days for a whole month where my royalty was zero."—K.A. Gandy, Dystopian author

When creating goals, start small and clearly define what you want. Perhaps you want to pay a specific bill in your household every month from your royalties, or maybe you'd like to pay for one of your kid's after-school activities.

Then scale up to the next level. Perhaps you want to pay for your weekly groceries, a car payment, or your family's annual vacation.

When you start seeing success, consider whether to set bigger challenges. Alternatively, if your first goal seems to be too much of a stretch, scale back to something more achievable while you work to see what parts of your business model you can improve.

5. MAKE IT HAPPEN

"I used to really believe in making S.M.A.R.T (small, measurable, achievable, realistic, time-bound) goals, but I've changed to something more simplistic. I set a huge, unrealistic goal. Then I backtrack to all the steps along the way it takes to get there and make small, bite-sized goals. The big goal is something more than six months out. The bite-sized can be achieved in around one to two months."—A.W. Scott, Romance author

As we mentioned in step one, the "how" will come much easier once you have worked out your "why." It's often one of the first things author coaches will ask in a session. If you cannot answer why you want to self-publish, then the process for how to best grow your business becomes cloudy and unclear. It can be frustrating when you are wading through molasses to reach a vague and nonspecific target that you're not even sure you want—or need—to hit.

Everyone's goals are different; therefore, the methods they use to achieve their goals will be different too. However, anyone can take certain steps to reach their goals.

If your goal is to earn a set monthly amount, you can easily calculate how much you need to hit per day to make it happen. From there, look at the tools in your author arsenal and decide which would be best suited to help you get to where you need to be, such as paid ads, newsletter swaps, Facebook group posts, paid newsletters, or larger street teams to promote new releases.

Everything you try will always come down to analyzing the data you have for your business and testing what does and doesn't work for your specific situation. ■

Lasairiona McMaster

Want more resources on setting monetary goals? Business and finance magazines offer great tips for how small businesses can approach growth and goal-setting in a realistic, achievable way.

These articles from *Forbes Magazine* are a great place to start:

- "Four Ways To Break Through Your Fear And Self-Doubt"
- "Me And My Side Hustle: Nina Allwood"
- "4 Ways To Crush Your Growth Marketing Goals"

Tech Tools

Courtesy of IndieAuthorTools.com
Got a tool you love and want to share with us?
Submit a tool at IndieAuthorTools.com

Bookvault
https://bookvault.app/

If you want to sell print books on your website, check out Bookvault. This easy-to-use, print-on-demand solution is an online portal from Printondemand-worldwide. It integrates with Shopify and Woocommerce, allowing you to automatically fulfill any order and ship around the world.

Payhip
https://payhip.com/

Payhip is an easy-to-use platform that lets you sell digital content directly to readers. After creating a free account, enter your products and prices, and then connect Payhip to either your Stripe or PayPal account to receive the money. You'll get paid after every transaction as it happens. Payhip's transaction fee is 5% on the free plan.

WooCommerce
https://woocommerce.com/

WooCommerce is a popular free plugin that lets you turn a WordPress website into an ecommerce store. It "makes creating and managing an online store simple, with reasonable levels of flexibility and several vital features such as inventory and tax management, secure payments, and shipping integration."

Shopify
https://www.shopify.com/

Shopify is a popular e-commerce platform that lets you create a customized online store. It is cloud-based and hosted, which means you don't have to maintain software or web servers. This provides "the flexibility to access and run your business from almost anywhere, including your mobile device."

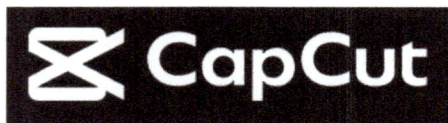

CapCut
https://www.capcut.com/

CapCut web is a free, easy-to-use video editor. No need for video editing experience. A variety of high-quality materials with copyright for commercial use are included. A mobile app is available for iOS and Android. CapCut and TikTok are owned by the same company, which created the tool to complement the popular platform's basic editing features.

Why We Need Disabled Stories (And How to Write Them)

As an individual with a rare chronic disease, I've centered my career in writing stories about disabled characters. Disabled people are everywhere, and they deserve to have their stories told—and not just those about their conditions.

It's not enough to make a story inclusive. Stories featuring disabled characters need to be just as colorful and immersing as books featuring able-bodied main characters. But how can authors effectively tell these stories without employing harmful stereotypes?

TERMINOLOGY AND INTENT MEANS EVERYTHING

Before diving into the details, it's essential to consider the terminology you use when writing about disability, including the difference between "disabled character" and "character with a disability."

The latter term focuses on referring to the character as a person first and their disability second, so the disability itself isn't what defines the character. However, "disabled" isn't a dirty word, and avoiding the phrase "disabled character" implies that it is.

It is understandable to want to avoid labels. However, a person can choose to have more than one label. A person can be a wife, but they can also be a CEO, a reader, and a volunteer. Disability is a singular factor of a character's experience, but it shouldn't be seen as the primary defining trait.

Overall, these two terms should be used interchangeably. If you are an able-bodied person who errs on the side of caution, "character with a disability" is typically a fine choice.

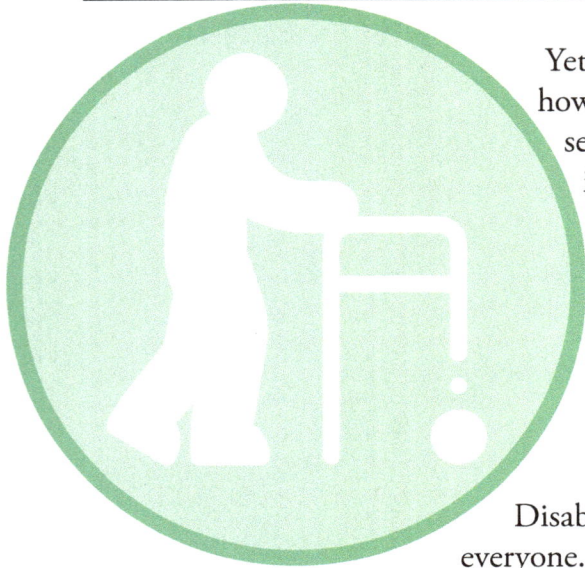

Yet it is important not to dictate to disabled writers how they may refer to their characters and themselves. Disability isn't just a diagnosis; for many, it is an identity, and policing how people identify and see themselves is both harmful and disrespectful. As with all writing, the words you use matter.

WHY WRITING DISABLED CHARACTERS IS IMPORTANT

Disability is a scale, and it looks different for everyone. To categorize someone only as "disabled" or "non-disabled" leaves no room for those who exist within gray areas. A person who has major clinical depression experiences disability differently than someone who is quadriplegic. But to refer to someone as being more or less able-bodied than someone else is unhelpful, as disabilities can look different on different people. Many invisible illnesses allow a person to appear able-bodied to the naked eye yet can have a significant impact on their lives.

Disabled people are people, and they have lives that are similar to able-bodied individuals. The key differences usually come down to issues of accessibility and prejudice. When writing about disabled characters, disability should not be the focus of the story. That is, of course, unless you are specifically writing a disability story about the main character's illness, but in this chronically ill author's opinion, books like these have been done to death. Disabled people don't want to read about themselves being sick. We want to read about disabled people being heroes, interacting with their world, and having extraordinary experiences.

In much of modern media, disability is portrayed as a negative experience. Disabled people die at the end, they suffer through much of the story, and a huge part of their character is based on nothing more than their diagnosis. But disability doesn't inherently have to be negative. It can be a neutral trait of the individual's experience, something they live with rather than struggle against.

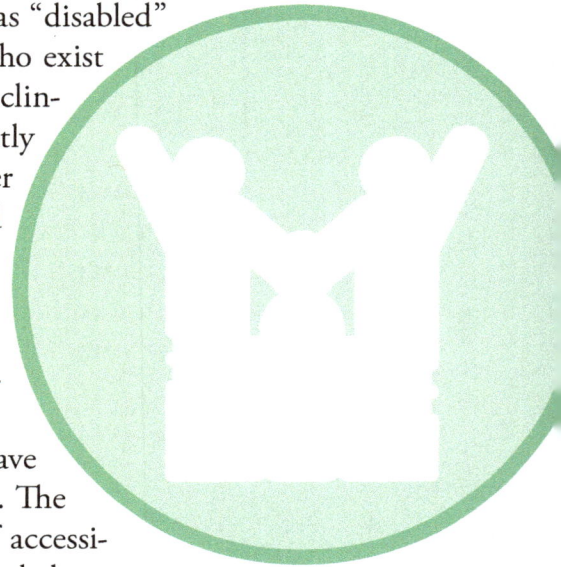

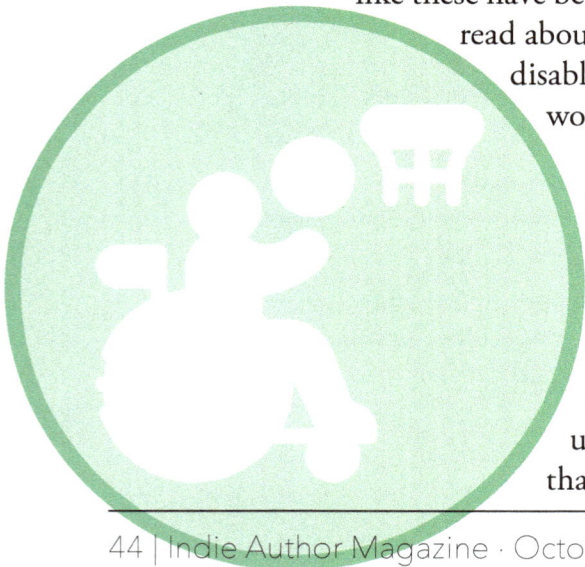

The point of writing disabled characters is to normalize them. Disabled people are not "others." They exist—making up as much as 15 percent of the population, according to the World Bank Group, a global partnership of institutions that works to create sustainable environments for marginalized communities. Disabled people lead interesting lives, and they have thoughts and feelings just as much as the able-bodied population does. And writing—and reading—about these characters gives disabled people representation, as well as helps able-bodied people better understand what the disabled experience is like.

As I've told friends, my illness is just "a thing"—something that is a part of my life that I handle just as I would any other piece. It's not "a deal"—something that has such a negative effect on my life that it becomes the focus of my existence.

HOW TO WRITE DISABLED CHARACTERS

Before attempting to begin your novel, research is key. It's not enough to understand the medical know-how of a person's diagnosis—an author must immerse themselves in learning about what life with that diagnosis is like.

To start, contact and gather information from organizations that advocate for people with disabilities. For example, the Immune Deficiency Foundation website would be helpful for learning more about immune-related disabilities. From there, many organizations have information about the disease itself, as well as educational materials and information about living with certain disorders.

For me, one of the most helpful ways to research various disabilities is by spending time in both virtual and physical spaces where people with that particular condition gather. There's only so much you can learn from a medical article online, and these formal documents often barely scratch the surface of the disabled experience. Instead, search for a meetup, convention, or online space for disabled people where you can participate as an observer. The knowledge you will receive will be golden. Many of these meet-up events can be found on the aforementioned websites.

While listening—and it is important that you listen, first and foremost—to these individuals talk with one another about their lives and experiences, you will gain a more accurate picture of their diagnosis than you ever could by listening to a physician speak on the subject. One-on-one interviews are crucial too. It's important to get time to talk to disabled people about their illnesses, so you can ask questions relating to your characters and your book. Many disabled people are comfortable speaking about their illness and are happy to answer respectful questions about it, such as the challenges they face while being disabled or how being disabled has changed their lives unexpectedly. Not all disabled experiences are detrimental—in my experience, I've found many aspects of my disability have affected my life positively, such as helping me to foster a more inclusive and patient mindset for myself and others.

Avoid implying that disabled people are inspirational, stronger than others, or brave for facing life with a condition. Disabled people can be inspirational and strong, but it can be detrimental for disabled people to hear others say that they wouldn't be able to handle living with a disability. Also avoid implying that a disabled person must struggle with a certain activity—many disabled people can do most of the things an able-bodied person can, as long as they are provided with the proper accommodations.

Group meetups can also be wonderful places to find sensitivity readers—readers who identify with the condition of your character and can point out any misconceptions in your novel during editing. At the end of the event or after a one-on-one interview, ask if that individual would be willing to be a sensitivity reader for you after you've finished writing, and offer to pay them for their time and knowledge.

Avoid hiring sensitivity readers who are caregivers of the disabled person and don't live with the diagnosis themselves. It's critical to understand that if you don't have that particular diagnosis, you will never know what it is like to live with that disability. Conversely, understand that disability has some universal experiences. Many disabled people struggle with accessibility in public spaces or experience discrimination as a result of being disabled. Most have experience with struggling to attain medical care or with getting doctors to take their symptoms seriously.

We are all human. We all have feelings and emotions, and despite the differences our bodies may present, the idea of humanity grounds us all. Above all, when writing disabled characters, keep in mind that they are, above all else, characters—ones you may have more in common with than you think.

RESOURCES AUTHORS MAY USE TO BEGIN RESEARCH:

U.S. Access Board: A list of disability research resources, including statistics on disability, primarily in the United States. https://access-board.gov/research/other.html

Charity Navigator: A list of all nonprofit organizations where authors can research the credibility and funding of a disability advocacy organization, as well as locate charities focused on individual conditions. https://charitynavigator.org

We Need Diverse Books: A website providing information and education on a variety of diverse books, mostly centered around children's fiction, some on disability. https://diversebooks.org

Megan Linski-Fox

Podcasts We Love

So Money with Farnoosh Torabi
https://podcasts.apple.com/us/podcast/
so-money-with-farnoosh-torabi/id955939085?mt=2

Award-winning financial journalist Farnoosh Torabi interviews financial leaders, authors, and influencers "about their financial perspectives, money failures, and habits" on So Money on CNET. The show updates every two days, and on Fridays, Torabi answers money questions from listeners.

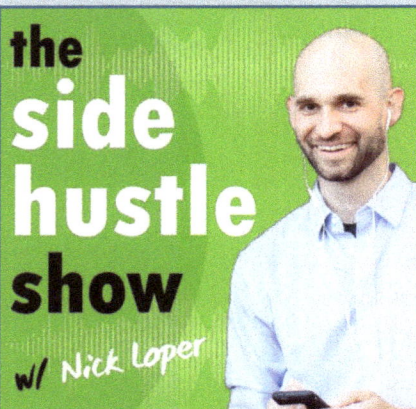

The Side Hustle Show
https://podcasts.apple.com/us/podcast/the-side-hustle-show/id655135292

Is self-publishing a side hustle for you? Join Nick Loper of Side Hustle Nation for high-value content to help you make extra money. The weekly show is a top-rated podcast with more than 500 episodes, featuring actionable tips and business strategies from successful entrepreneurs.

Smart Passive Income
https://podcasts.apple.com/us/podcast/the-smart-passive-income-online-business-and/id383084001

Pat Flynn, creator of the Smart Passive Income blog, reveals "his online business and blogging strategies, income sources, and killer marketing tips and tricks" on this podcast. Join entrepreneur and author Flynn weekly for a combo of interviews, co-hosts, and solo shows.

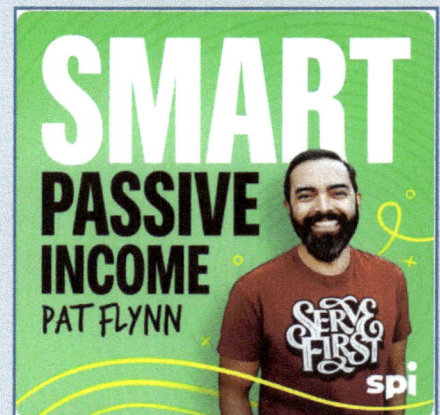

Food for Thought

ADD FLAVOR TO YOUR FICTION WITH THESE TECHNIQUES FOR WRITING ABOUT FOOD

Adam and Eve had their fateful apple. Tales of the Old West had chuck wagons. The Jetsons had food pellets. No matter what genre you're writing in, if your story contains living beings and plays out over more than a day or two, you're going to have to feed and water your characters.

Tales of epic journeys can be a lot of fun to write, but they also need to ring true, or your readers will devour you in their reviews. Your job as a writer is to get them to suspend their disbelief, not to insult their intelligence by asking them to believe that a quart of milk would still be drinkable after a week in the backpack of a character stumbling their way across the desert. Fortunately, with a little research and pre-planning, you can serve up a delicious tale that leaves your readers hungry for more.

FEAST AND FAMINE

Life's basic necessities like food and shelter aren't too difficult to deal with when your characters have the luxury of a fully stocked and functional home base, but things can get a little dicey when you toss in a road trip or a cataclysmic event like an apocalypse or an alien invasion.

Even if your story takes place in a modern day setting, it's important to pay attention to how often your characters eat and what they're eating. It may also be worth noting that the need to sustain your characters doesn't apply only to human characters—it also applies to pets and magical creatures. A good rule of thumb here is to treat all your character's needs with the same level of urgency and caution.

The average person needs approximately 1,200 calories per day to maintain long-term health, but that number increases as your character's level of physical activity increases. So too does the need for water. Adult bodies are approximately 60 percent water, while children's bodies are closer to 75 percent water. Keeping your characters adequately hydrated is essential to their health and survival. The FEMA website offers a great resource for determining how much your characters need to eat and drink, as well as information on how they should store their stockpile: https://fema.gov/pdf/library/f&web.pdf.

Research is especially important when working in historical settings. Be sure to verify that the foods your characters are eating are actually possible for the time period. The Food Timeline at https://foodtimeline.org can be a great resource for this—the database offers information on the evolution of food throughout history, including locations, time periods, and archived recipes for dishes.

LAWS OF SCIENCE

Beyond knowing what your characters eat, one of the first things you need to consider when dealing with food on a long journey is how the physical world affects your ability to acquire and prepare it. Let's say you're penning the next great space opera, and your characters have just landed on some distant planet. Before they rush out to gather wood so they can roast space shrimp

to celebrate, consider whether those materials would be available—or even whether the atmosphere would allow for a fire. Pay the same level of attention to the animals your characters hunt, trap, or catch, as well as the plants they consume. If the animals or plants seem out of place given your character's physical location or climate, your readers will notice.

FOOD SAFETY

For those in the commercial food industry, the Hazard Analysis and Critical Control Points (HACCP) principles are "an internationally recognized method of identifying and managing food safety related risk," according to the Safe Food Alliance. Although you probably don't need to be so thorough as an author, you really should be familiar with food safety basics—otherwise you might end up killing your characters long before they reach their destination.

Food sustains us, but it can also do us dirty if we aren't careful with how we store and handle it. In the culinary world, the temperature range referred to as the danger zone spans 40 degrees Fahrenheit to 140 degrees Fahrenheit. In this range, bacteria can grow at a rapid rate and cause a host of ugly, painful foodborne illnesses.

Unless your story takes place in Siberia or the scorching-hot surface of Venus, it's likely that your characters will spend most of their journey or their day-to-day life somewhere within the danger zone temperature range, and it will impact the way they deal with food. For stories that involve travel, it might be best to avoid dairy and uncooked meats, as these spoil easily and quickly. Grain-based, packaged, or processed foods that don't require cooking or cold storage are usually a safe bet for keeping your characters fed when they're on the move.

Knowing what kinds of foods are available and how to store them safely is great when it comes to protecting your characters; however, that's not to say that you should always play it safe. Sometimes a story calls for characters to embrace the dark side, and offering up a flask of contaminated water or applying a savory spice rub to cover up the scent of spoiled meat just might be the tastiest way to slow down or take out an enemy. ■

Jenn Mitchell

Poetry by the Book

As a gorgeous art form that has survived the centuries and that readers around the globe admire and revere, poetry can be more like music than a storytelling genre, with stanzas and word choice providing a unique cadence to access the poet's soul. These rhythmic works come in a myriad of styles, length, and even interpretation, but they should always remain true to the heart of the writer.

In writing a poetry collection, write from the depths of your soul, and your readers will connect. Not every poem is for every reader, nor is every collection, but avid consumers of collections will flock to yours if you follow that golden rule. Still, there are other expectations that will help draw readers to your work, from collection length to the types of poems you include. Although they're not a requirement, these elements are important to understand as you consider whether you're ready to share your own soul with the world.

POETRY TYPE

When writing, poets often tarry over length or rhyme, but neither of these is as important as the words themselves. The same is true when preparing to publish. You may choose rhymes, no rhymes, or even write free verse—prose in the form of poetry, and one of the more popular types of modern poetry—when building your collection.

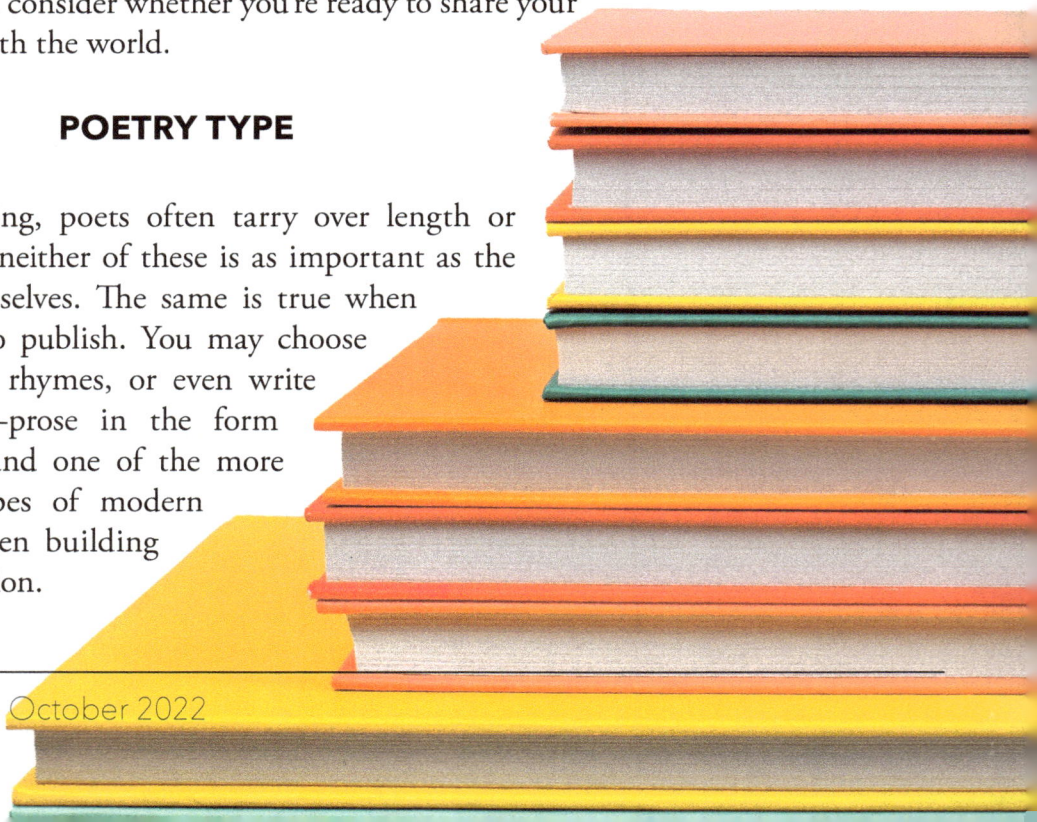

WHAT TO CONSIDER BEFORE SELF-PUBLISHING YOUR COLLECTION

When constructing a poem, most poets stick to having each line being approximately the same length, which works well for meter. This can also make your work easier to format for publication, but again, nothing is required, so make the choice you feel suits your art best.

THEME

When selecting poems to include in a collection, it's best to decide on a theme or overarching message for your work. You might choose love, death, or anything in between. Rupi Kaur's collection *milk and honey* deals with pain. The best-selling work is divided into four chapters, each containing poems on different types of pain. This is a structure that suits many poetry collections well, and by sorting your poems into groups, parts, or chapters, you can create an expectation among your readers regarding what they'll find in those poems. Alternatively, you can arrange your poetry so your collection tells a story from one poem to the next, similar to a novel in verse.

LENGTH

In choosing your poems, do not concern yourself with choosing all the same style or even lengths of poetry. Many collections have various styles of poems within the pages; some may rhyme, and some may be free verse. However, you'll want to consider how to order the poems based on length. If you have a poem that lasts a few pages while all your others are contained on a single page, consider putting that poem toward the back of the collection. Some poets include short stories among the pages of poetry, which is also acceptable, but the same rule applies. Move that short story to the back of the collection.

The length of the collection itself is up to you. Most stay around 80 to 120 pages, but some chapbooks contain only twelve pages, while longer collections can be around two hundred pages. If writing a novel in verse, the page range can be upwards of three hundred pages. Because it's poetry, it is up to each individual poet how many pages you need in order for the reader to fully experience your theme.

As you're considering the length of your pieces, decide also whether any of your pieces will require a more artistic layout. Some poets include illustrations alongside their poems, as Kaur does. Poems may also have different shapes through creative formatting, which provides a unique feeling for that poem. Depending on the complexity of the design and your experience level, you might need to hire an interior designer to help format your work the way you want it to appear. And when it comes time to publish, the blog for the editing platform Reedsy (https://blog.reedsy.com) has underlined additional information on things you can do to market your poetry, including live readings, using social media, and entering contests.

Of course, these are all just suggestions. And for as many expectations exist within a given genre, there are always just as many exceptions to the rules. Experiment with some of these ideas in order to make something that is all your own. In the end, as long as you follow your heart and soul in your poetry, you'll find there is little you can do wrong. ◼

Angie Martin

Step-by-Step Success

ACHIEVE THE WORK-LIFE BALANCING ACT A LITTLE BIT AT A TIME

An author's career is a long game. Life-changing success rarely comes after writing one or two books. Whether you're publishing a book every month or every year, keeping to your schedule is the best way to meet your goals. But are you also accommodating your lifestyle goals in the process?

In the short term, we can work every waking hour. But is that why you became a writer? Or did you picture yourself spending more time with your family? Did you want more flexibility and freedom?

I'm guessing you didn't want to be a slave to your writing. Or maybe your life took an unexpected turn and you're struggling to keep up your earlier pace.

The secret is not to set yourself up for failure. Building a buffer in your life is a great way to succeed at all your goals.

If you're looking to create more flexibility and space in your life, consider the following:

1. How much time do you have to dedicate to your work each day, week, and month?
2. How much time will you spend with your family, on vacation, traveling, or on your other lifestyle goals?
3. Do you have any health issues that flare up?

When setting and implementing boundaries, success is not just your goal. It's your secret weapon. Successes large and small give your body a dopamine hit and are highly motivating.

Structure your goals and break them down into small pieces for quick wins that build momentum. Create annual goals, quarterly goals, monthly goals, weekly goals, daily goals, and even hourly goals—however granular you need to get so you can get those successes and those dopamine hits. Small steps that make up larger steps will get you to your end goal. ◼

— Alice Briggs

The Silent Struggle

THE AUTHOR'S SELF-CARE GUIDE FOR A HEALTHIER MIND

As always, if you suffer from mental illness, these tips are not in lieu of seeking proper professional treatment. If you are in immediate danger of suicidal thoughts or tendencies, please contact the National Suicide Hotline at 988, call a local hotline, contact 911 to have an ambulance sent to your location, or seek immediate treatment at the closest emergency room. You can contact the National Alliance on Mental Illness at 800-950-NAMI (6264) or live chat with someone on its website, https://nami.org.

When dealing with mental illness, it's often hard to power through the low points, let alone write your next book. But there are several things you can focus on during these times, as well as every day, to bring normalcy to your life as much as possible.

The National Institute on Mental Health recommends placing self-care first. Place the oxygen mask on yourself before helping others. This may seem difficult if you have a family who depends on you, but if you've not cared for your own mental health needs, caring for others can be quite the task.

Self-care looks different with mental health. Eating right, exercising, and getting enough sleep are at the top of the self-care list. Ensure you always take your medications on time, and seek professional help as needed.

Don't force yourself to write a certain amount each day, unless that is one of your coping mechanisms. Set small, attainable goals or tasks to accomplish, such as writing five hundred words or editing only a chapter or two. Everyone has different methods of dealing with stress, so find the way that helps you most. "I meditate and read positive sayings daily," says one author with anxiety, who spoke on a condition of anonymity. "If I become too overwhelmed, I go straight to my bath, where I relax with bubbles, candles, and a good book."

Focusing on positivity is important. Avoid the news if it causes you any stress, and keep in touch with family and friends for support and a kind word.

No matter which mental health issues are in your life, there are many tricks to keeping your mind healthy. Your therapist can help you find new ways to cope daily while you continue to write amazing works.

This is the third and final article in a series of articles discussing mental illness and the role it can play in an author's career. ■

Angie Martin

20 Essentials for 20Books Vegas

Fast Flowing Spou

Secure Lid Lock

Easy Measurement Counter

Ahead of 20Books Vegas, the annual four-day indie author conference hosted by 20BooksTo50K® creator Craig Martelle, a renewed era of travel has arrived—and it's safe to say it's more inconvenient than ever. In 2022, long lines, delays, and short staffing have all contributed to higher levels of stress and frustration as travelers return to in-person event attendance. With only a month left before one of the largest self-publishing conferences in the world, what's an author to do?

We've been to 20Books Vegas before, so we've learned all the tricks and hacks that you need for the best conference experience. Although we're not magically able to find extra planes, seats, or staff to ease the new reality of travel frustration, we can offer you a list of twenty products and travel hacks to make the trip a bit easier as you head to Las Vegas this November. From apps that offer added benefits to spritzes and serums to soothe your skin and ways to save time and money when you're onsite, these are your must-haves for hitting the road once again.

Individual products are available on Amazon via the links provided, or view the complete list at https://amazon.com/shop/chellehoniker. If you buy something using links in our stories, we may earn a commission. This helps support our magazine, but it won't cost you anything extra.

BREEZE THROUGH THE AIRPORT

Planning should start with a Swiss Army tool to carry it all, and you'll find it in this backpack: https://amzn.to/3LvUv8F. The three-compartment layout means your electronics can remain cushioned in the center for easy access during airport security.

Other handy features include a spot to tuck your glasses, a water bottle pocket, a luggage sleeve so the backpack fits over your carry-on bag, a built-in USB port on the outside—you can keep your portable charging battery inside and your mobile device tethered outside—and an RFID shield to keep your scannable passport information from any bad guys trolling the airport.

Stay warm, stylish, and organized while thwarting pickpockets with these infinity scarves (black infinity scarf: https://amzn.to/3f9QBWY; plaid infinity scarf: https://amzn.to/3BZEjcF), which have a hidden zippered pocket to keep your valuables handy. The pocket is big enough for your mobile phone, boarding pass, and wallet, ensuring safe and easy access to what you need.

Slide through security without drama (llama) with these cute animal-themed compression socks: https://amzn.to/3LFaDVy. On long flights, compression garments can prevent ankle swelling and reduce the risk of blood clots often attributed to sitting for long periods of time, according to physicians at the University of Texas Health Science Center at Houston.

(DON'T) STAY THIRSTY, FRIENDS

Studies show that flying causes dehydration and zaps your energy, according to the Cleveland Clinic. Keeping water on hand is a surefire way to combat the problem.

This water bottle (https://amzn.to/3qVhMY3) is the perfect size for sipping often during long sessions and can be filled from the many hydration stations in airports and conference common areas. The flip top also locks securely to prevent spills.

Pro Tip: Clean and disinfect your bottle overnight with denture cleaning tablets to prevent bacteria and biofilm.

Another tip from frequent fliers? Don't forget your electrolytes. "Electrolytes are minerals found in your blood that help regulate and control the balance of fluids in the body," according to the Cleveland Clinic. "These minerals play a role in regulating blood pressure, muscle contraction and keep your system functioning properly." These packets (https://amzn.to/3fcTdmI) keep the wonder powder dry until you're ready to tap it into your water bottle and give it a shake.

SPRUCE UP BETWEEN SESSIONS

Interacting in public means talking, and you should be prepared to do a lot of it over the four days of 20Books Vegas. In case your voice starts to get strained, keep some of these Throat Coat lozenges handy (https://amzn.to/3DIEyKk) and stash this lip balm (https://amzn.to/3r3iZwp) in one of your backpack pockets.

Of course, in a post-COVID world, you'll need hand sanitizer (https://amzn.to/3xDBQlp) and a place to store it. Use one of these hand sanitizer holders (https://amzn.to/3xDBQlp) to carry it securely clipped to your backpack.

Dragon breath after the afternoon coffee break? Nip into the washroom and freshen your mouth with these small toothbrush alternatives called Wisps (https://amzn.to/3BZfTQB). They're more effective than endlessly popping breath mints.

While you're there, dab a little of this unscented Lume Deodorant where it's needed (https://amzn.to/3BsMNr6) and give yourself a little wake-up call with this spritz water (https://amzn.to/3xESv8w). It's cooling, soothing, and combats the drying effects of the sub-zero air conditioning at the conference.

TAKE YOUR NETWORKING TO THE NEXT LEVEL

Although plenty of 20Books-goers opt to bring a full-sized laptop, it's far more efficient to just carry your iPad, phone, or tablet to sessions for note-taking. This Bluetooth keyboard (https://amzn.to/3BZMPZh) connects and sets your tablet in the right position to type significant notes, and it comes with a spot for an Apple Pencil or stylus for handwritten notes, if you prefer.

Pro Tip: If you're using a phone or tablet to take notes during a session, the Evernote app, available for Apple and Android users, will allow you to download the presenter's PDF slides and mark them up digitally, as well as take photos of anything presented during the session for one complete record.

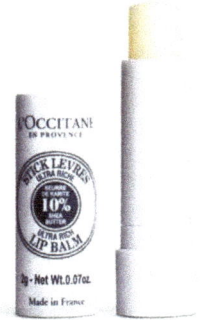

Worried about germs, or just don't want the hassle of physical business cards? Here's a touchless alternative. With POPL, add your contact information to the app in a secure profile, and then connect a contact with a tap or a QR code scan. You can also purchase devices like a sticky disk on the back of your phone, keychains, wrist badges, or metallic cards.

Pro Tip: Use https://popl.co/?ref=indieauthormagazine and get 20 percent off with the coupon code: IndieAuthor

GET A GOOD NIGHT'S SLEEP …

Being away from home can lead to insomnia. Combat that with some pampering before bed to wind down—and remember that self-care has no gender. Start with removing the travel grime with these moisturizing cleansing cloths (https://amzn.to/3RaRdIZ), and then dab some eye cream (https://amzn.to/3dvF2Jk) to reduce puffiness. Finish with this great vitamin C face serum (https://amzn.to/3fcVcYc), and you're ready to catch some z's.

Still can't sleep? Tune out any ambient noise and light with an eye mask that doubles as a pair of Bluetooth headphones (https://amzn.to/3S2R77J). This model is designed for side sleepers and can be more comfortable than others on the market.

Pro Tip: Pair with the Calm app, available on Google Play and the Apple App Store, to tell you a sleep story, and you're guaranteed to wake refreshed and ready for the next conference day.

… OR PLENTY OF CAFFEINE

Whether it's jet lag or a late night of conference shenanigans the night before, some people will still need a caffeine boost to make it out of their hotel room. Many hotels in Las Vegas do not offer a coffee maker in their rooms—they want you out and spending money on food and beverage in their establishments. Fortunately, we've got some ideas to try instead.

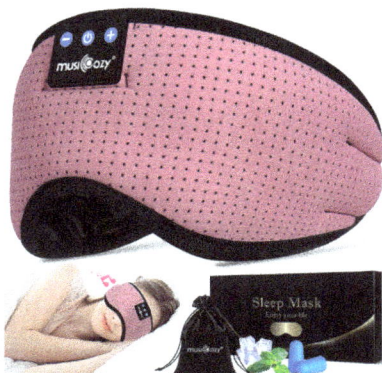

This folding kettle (https://amzn.to/3xJzVMt) fits inconspicuously in any size bag and heats water in a snap before collapsing back down to travel size once again when you're headed home. It's perfect for several "cuppas," but if you're traveling solo, there's a smaller solution in this heated travel mug (https://amzn.to/3BCUET6).

If you're a coffee lover, try this handheld espresso maker (https://amzn.to/3f5s3hD) for your morning brew. This machine uses small Nespresso pods and produces espresso shots with a few pumps of pressure and the hot water from your kettle. Our list includes three different flavors and strengths of pods to get you your wake-up juice for under one dollar per cup: Angelino's Bold (https://amzn.to/3Uw4kHG); Café Bustelo (https://amzn.to/3LFdj5y), and Lavazza (https://amzn.to/3BZRM4j).

Pro Tip: Lavazza also has a location inside the Bally's Event Center, where 20Books Vegas is held. Visit their location throughout the day for an extra energy boost—after you've visited the infamous cake machine, of course.

With some careful planning and these secret weapons, you're bound to have a great 20Books Vegas experience. We'll see you there!

Have a product you love to use for your conference travels that's not on this list? Let us know! We may feature it in future issues. Email: suggestions@indieauthormagazine.com ◼

Chelle Honiker

Conference Fashion from Suze

Suze Solari is an image consultant and fashion author. She helps her clients look and feel amazing, plus have an empowered closet they love, so they always show up on brand with confidence, joy.

Here are her four fashion picks for conference-goers to blend comfort and style

MEN:

- Stretchy Knit Blazer + fitted graphic T-shirt: Italian Knit Blazer | Bonobos
- Upscale Sneaker, all white or gray: adidas Daily 3.0 Sneaker–Men's | DSW

WOMEN:

- Suede or stretchy easy Moto jacket: https://athleta.gap.com/browse/product.do?pid=982849032
- Upscale platform sneaker: https://www.dsw.com/en/us/product/new-balance-fresh-foam-x70-sneaker—-womens/517576?activeColor=512

The strategies she teaches include removing from clients' closets what doesn't serve them; maximizing their wardrobe investment by creating go-to outfits so they always know what to wear for events, photo shoots, and travel, saving precious time and money.

She has many levels where she can help, incuding 1:1 Private Client work, Group Program, and five handbooks on style.

Visit her website and view all the latest style content: https://linktr.ee/SuzeSolari

From the Stacks

Courtesy of IndieAuthorTools.com
Got a book you love and want to share with us?
Submit a book at IndieAuthorTools.com

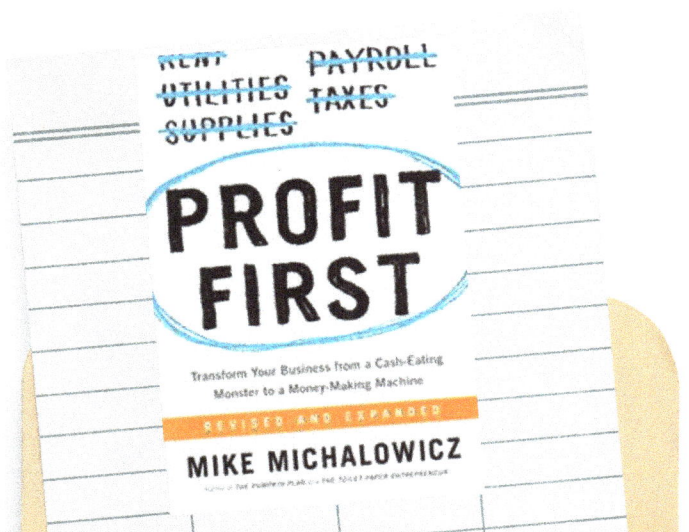

Profit First: Transform Your Business from a Cash-Eating Monster to a Money-Making Machine

https://books2read.com/u/3J6Ege

Just as the most effective weight loss strategy is to limit portions by using smaller plates, [serial entrepreneur Mike] Michalowicz shows that by taking profit first and apportioning only what remains for expenses, entrepreneurs will transform their businesses from cash-eating monsters to profitable cash cows.

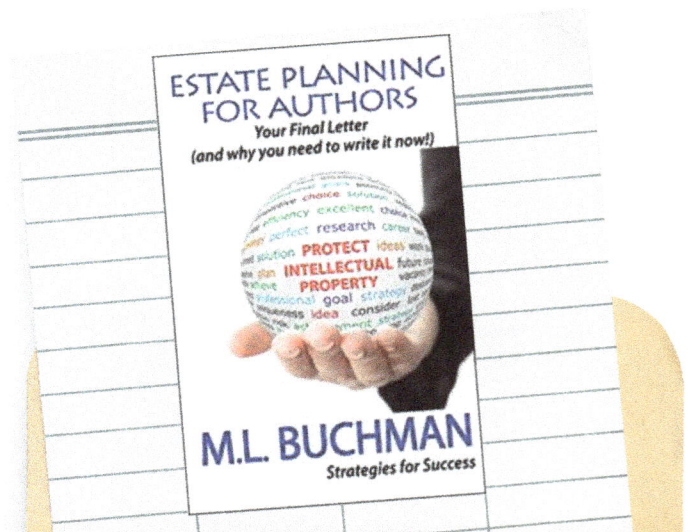

Estate Planning for Authors: Your Final Letter

https://books2read.com/u/bxJ156

The challenge with an estate that includes Intellectual Property (books, stories, plays, films, etc.), is it has a value that can last another 70 years after your death. [Estate Planning for Authors: Your Final Letter] is a practical guide for educating your heir on … what they've just received and what their options are to manage it.

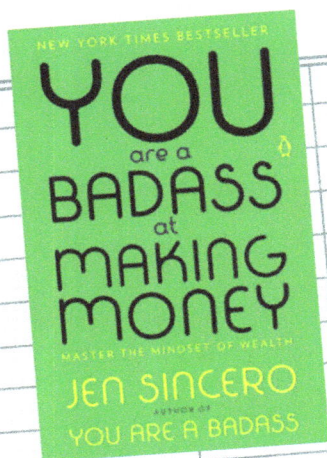

You Are a Badass at Making Money: Master the Mindset of Wealth
https://books2read.com/u/boy2d9

You Are a Badass at Making Money will launch you past the fears and stumbling blocks that have kept financial success beyond your reach. Drawing on her own transformation over just a few years from a woman living in a converted garage with tumbleweeds blowing through her bank account to a woman who travels the world in style, Jen Sincero … combines hilarious personal essays with bite-size, aha concepts that unlock earning potential and get real results.

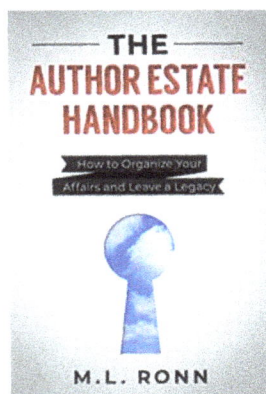

The Author Estate Handbook: How to Organize Your Affairs and Leave a Legacy
https://books2read.com/u/md162w

The Author Estate Handbook "will help you get your affairs in order, understand estate planning basics, and make a plan so that you can create a legacy that will continue making money for your family long after you're gone."

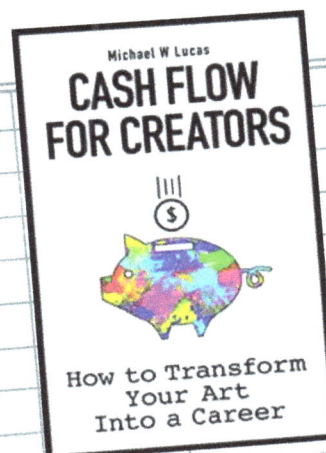

Cash Flow for Creators: How to Transform Your Art Into a Career
https://books2read.com/u/3nX599

Cash Flow For Creators provides a map and a flashlight for building an artistic business from the ground up. … In the bewildering torrent of business rules, which matter to a creator — and which don't? *Cash Flow for Creators* has you covered, and tells you the secret no other business book will: Business is easier than art once someone explains the rules and tells you how to win.

In This Issue

Executive Team

Chelle Honiker, Publisher

As the publisher of Indie Author Magazine, Chelle Honiker brings nearly three decades of startup, technology, training, and executive leadership experience to the role. She's a serial entrepreneur, founding and selling multiple successful companies including a training development company, travel agency, website design and hosting firm, a digital marketing consultancy, and a wedding planning firm. She's organized and curated multiple TEDx events and hired to assist other nonprofit organizations as a fractional executive, including The Travel Institute and The Freelance Association.

As a writer, speaker, and trainer she believes in the power of words and their ability to heal, inspire, incite, and motivate. Her greatest inspiration is her daughters, Kelsea and Cathryn, who tolerate her tendency to run away from home to play with her friends around the world for months at a time. It's said she could run a small country with just the contents of her backpack.

Alice Briggs, Creative Director

As the creative director of Indie Author Magazine, Alice Briggs utilizes her more than three decades of artistic exploration and expression, business startup adventures, and leadership skills. A serial entrepreneur, she has started several successful businesses. She brings her experience in creative direction, magazine layout and design, and graphic design in and outside of the indie author community to her role.

With a masters of science in Occupational Therapy, she has a broad skill set and uses it to assist others in achieving their desired goals. As a writer, teacher, healer, and artist, she loves to see people accomplish all they desire. She's excited to see how IAM will encourage many authors to succeed in whatever way they choose. She hopes to meet many of you in various places around the world once her passport is back in use.

Nicole Schroeder, Editor in Chief

Nicole Schroeder is a storyteller at heart. As the editor in chief of Indie Author Magazine, she brings nearly a decade of journalism and editorial experience to the publication, delighting in any opportunity to tell true stories and help others do the same. She holds a bachelor's degree from the Missouri School of Journalism and minors in English and Spanish. Her previous work includes editorial roles at local publications, and she's helped edit and produce numerous fiction and nonfiction books, including a Holocaust survivor's memoir, alongside independent publishers. Her own creative writing has been published in national literary magazines. When she's not at her writing desk, Nicole is usually in the saddle, cuddling her guinea pigs, or spending time with family. She loves any excuse to talk about Marvel movies and considers National Novel Writing Month its own holiday.

Writers

Gill Fernley

Gill Fernley writes fiction in several genres under different pen names, but what all of them have in common is humour and romance, because she can't resist a happy ending or a good laugh. She's also a freelance content writer and has been running her own business since 2013. Before that, she was a technical author and documentation manager for an engineering company and can describe to you more than you'd ever wish to know about airflow and filtration in downflow booths. Still awake? Wow, that's a first! Anyway, that experience taught her how to explain complex things in straightforward language and she hopes it will come in handy for writing articles for IAM. Outside of writing, she's a cake decorator, expert shoe hoarder, and is fluent in English, dry humour and procrastibaking.

Megan Linski-Fox

Megan Linski lives in Michigan. She is a USA TODAY Bestselling Author and the author of more than fifty novels. She has over fifteen years of experience writing books alongside working as a journalist and editor. She graduated from the University of Iowa, where she studied Creative Writing.

Megan advocates for the rights of the disabled, and is an activist for mental health awareness. She co-writes the Hidden Legends Universe with Alicia Rades. She also writes under the pen name of Natalie Erin for the Creatures of the Lands series, co-authored by Krisen Lison.

Craig Martelle

High school Valedictorian enlists in the Marine Corps under a guaranteed tank contract. An inauspicious start that was quickly superseded by excelling in language study. Contract waived, a year at the Defense Language Institute to learn Russian and off to keep my ears on the big red machine during the Soviet years. Back to DLI for advanced Russian after reenlisting. Deploying. Then getting selected to get a commission. Earned a four-year degree in two years by majoring in Russian Language. It was a cop out, but I wanted to get back to the fleet. One summa cum laude graduation later, that's where I found myself. My first gig as a second lieutenant was on a general staff. I did well enough that I stayed at that level or higher for the rest of my career, while getting some choice side gigs – UAE, Bahrain, Korea, Russia, and Ukraine.

Major Martelle. I retired from the Marines after a couple years at the embassy in Moscow working arms control issues. The locals called me The German, because of my accent in Russian. That worked for me. It kept me off the radar. Just until it didn't. Expelled after two years for activities inconsistent with my diplomatic status, I went to Ukraine. Can't let twenty years of Russian language go to waste. More arms control. More diplomatic stuff. Then 9/11 and off to war. That was enough deployment for me. Then came retirement.

Department of Homeland Security was a phenomenally miserable gig. I quit that job quickly enough and went to law school. A second summa cum laude later and I was working for a high-end consulting firm performing business diagnostics, business law, and leadership coaching. More deployments. For the money they paid me, I was good with that. Just until I wasn't. Then I started writing. You'll find Easter eggs from my career hidden within all my books. Enjoy the stories.

Angie Martin

Award-winning author Angie Martin has spent over a decade mentoring and helping new and experienced authors as they prepare to send their babies into the world. She relies on her criminal justice background and knack for researching the tiniest of details to assist others when crafting their own novels. She has given countless speeches in various aspects of writing, including creating characters, self-publishing, and writing supernatural and paranormal. She also assisted in leading a popular California writers' group, which organized several book signings for local authors. In addition to having experience in film, she created the first interactive murder mystery on Clubhouse and writes and directs each episode. Angie now resides in rural Tennessee, where she continues to help authors around the world in every stage of publication while writing her own thriller and horror books, as well as branching out into new genres.

Lasairiona McMaster

With a bachelor of arts in Politics and a minor in Culture and Media Studies, Lasairiona McMaster left the Emerald Isle for the great state of Texas and found her soul's home among queso and margaritas. When a decade of volunteering, expat and lifestyle blogging, and living abroad came to an end, she repatriated to Northern Ireland. Dusting off an old manuscript she'd penned in college, she hit the "publish" button in 2019, and hasn't looked back.

She writes relatable romance featuring themes of societal taboos, like male mental health, and that "just one book" is now a multi-series world that keeps growing.

When she's not in the writing cave, she's a professional nagger, developmental editor, and has mastered the art of making great friends from complete strangers. She's a left-handed Aquarian and enneagram four who loves to travel, sing, and never wears matching socks.

Jenn Mitchell

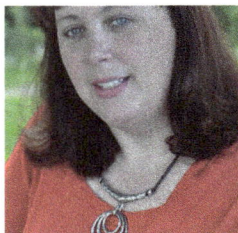

Jenn Mitchell writes Urban Fantasy and Weird West, as well as culinary cozy mysteries under the pen name, J Lee Mitchell. She writes, cooks, and gardens in the heart of South Central Pennsylvania's Amish Country. When she's not doing these things, she dreams of training llama riding ninjas.

She enjoys traveling, quilting, hoarding cookbooks, Sanntangling, and spending time with the World's most patient and loving significant other.

Susan Odev

Susan has banked over three decades of work experience in the fields of personal and organizational development, being a freelance corporate trainer and consultant alongside holding down "real" jobs for over twenty-five years. Specializing in entrepreneurial mindsets, she has written several non-fiction business books, once gaining a coveted Amazon #1 best seller tag in business and entrepreneurship, an accolade she now strives to emulate with her fiction.

Currently working on her fifth novel, under a top secret pen name, the craft and marketing aspects of being a successful indie author equally fascinate and terrify her.

A lover of history with a criminal record collection, Susan lives in a retro orange and avocado world. Once described by a colleague as being an "onion," Susan has many layers, as have ogres (according to Shrek). She would like to think this makes her cool, her teenage children just think she's embarrassing.

Joe Solari

Joe Solari is an author, entrepreneur, and consultant. Since 2016 he has been helping best-selling authors build great publishing businesses. He has worked to create tools and systems to help passionate business owners professionalize their team and operations to achieve exceptional results. Joe graduated with a BFA from the School of the Art Institute and an MBA from Chicago Booth School of Business. He has been an owner, investor, partner, and operator of numerous businesses. He lives in Illinois with his wife Suze, author of the T-Shirt & Jeans Handbook, and their two sons Rowan and Vincent.

MERCH FOR AUTHORS

Branded merch on Etsy, Amazon, and your own site.
Learn about extended stock licenses.
Includes sample contracts.

envatoelements

Travel & Hotel Email Builder
By theemon

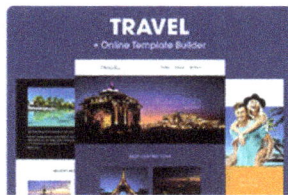

Travel Email Builder
By HyperPix

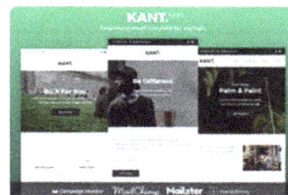

Kant - Email Template
By ThemeMountain

Olive - Fashion Email Template
By giantdesign

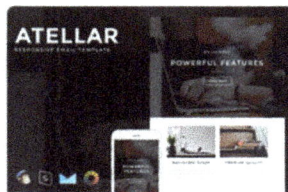

Metro App - Instapage Template
By Morad

ButaPest Email Template
By JeetuG

All the Email Templates you need and many other design elements, are available for a monthly subscription by subscribing to Envato Elements. The subscription costs $16.50 per month and gives you **unlimited access** to a massive and growing library of **1,500,000+** items that can be downloaded as often as you need (stock photos too)!

DOWNLOAD NOW

Ready to level up your indie author career?

Trick question.
Of course
you are.

*INDIE
^Author Tools

PUBLISHERROCKET

FIND
PROFITABLE
KINDLE
KEYWORDS

Book Marketing Research
Made Simple!

writelink.to/pubrocket

COME VISIT

the *Cake Machine* STAY for the *Conference.*

Las Vegas
Nevada
November
14-18, 2022

writelink.to/20Books

20 BOOKS
TO 50K®
A RISING TIDE LIFTS ALL BOATS